Thought this
might "come in
handy!"

Merry Christmas
"89"

Love
Mark
&
Jillie

# A DOG OWNER'S GUIDE TO

## American and English

# COCKER SPANIELS

Tetra Press

16023

# A DOG OWNER'S GUIDE TO

## American and English

# COCKER SPANIELS

### Frank Kane & Phyllis Wise
### Photographs by Marc Henrie

# A Salamander Book

# Contents

# Credits

Editor: Jo Finnis
Designer: Philip Gorton
Photographs: Marc Henrie
Illustrations: Ray Hutchins
Color origination: Rodney Howe Ltd
Typesetting: Rapidset, London
Printed in Portugal

# Photographer

Marc Henrie began his career as a Stills Man at the famous Ealing Film
Studios in London. He then moved to Hollywood where he worked for
MGM, RKO, Paramount and Warner Brothers, photographing the
Hollywood greats: Humphrey Bogart, Edward G Robinson, Gary Cooper,
Joan Crawford and Ingrid Bergman, to name a few. He was one of the last
photographers to photograph Marilyn Monroe. During this time, he was
in great demand to photograph the stars with their pets. Later, after he
had returned to England, Marc specialized in photographing dogs and
cats, rapidly establishing an international reputation. He has won
numerous photographic awards, most recently Kodak Award for the Best
Animal Photograph and the Neal Foundation Award for Outstanding
Photography of Animal Behaviour.
Marc is married to ex-ballet dancer, Fiona Henrie, who now writes and
illustrates books on animals. They live in West London with their daughter
Fleur, two Cavalier King Charles Spaniels and a cat called Topaz.

# Authors

**Phyllis Wise** and her late husband began breeding and showing English
Cocker Spaniels in 1950. In 1956 they bred their first Champion, Sh Ch
Astrawin Aphrodite, winner of 12 CCs and 12 Reserve CCs including Best
of Breed, Crufts 1961 and Best in Show at the Cocker Club Show, 1958.
Over the following 30 years, they bred seven more UK Champions, which
collectively won 50 CCs and almost 100 Reserve CCs. Amongst the many
UK and International Champions bred by Phyllis, Altesse Royale became
Cocker of the Year in Norway, while the famous Apollo was made Dog of
the Year All Breeds in Finland. There are few show-winning Cocker
Spaniels in Scandinavia which do not have one or other of these dogs in
their pedigrees.
Phyllis judged her first show in 1956 and has since judged regularly both
in the UK, including the Cocker Spaniel Club Show and Crufts, and
overseas.

**Frank Kane** has been showing dogs since his schooldays, and owned his
first American Cocker Spaniel in 1970. Frank is now owner of the
prestigious Hirontower affix kennels, and from that he has produced a
string of champions in the UK and overseas. He has also judged at many
shows around the world as well as in the UK, including Crufts Dog Show
in 1984.
Frank has also won success in the show ring with his Sealyham Terriers.

## Contributor

Richard G Beauchamp has contributed the chapter in Section Two on the
history of the American Cocker Spaniel – how the breed was established
and its subsequent development in the United States.
Richard Beauchamp, of the famous Beau Monde kennel, has been
involved with American Cockers since the early 1950s – the era often
referred to as the 'Golden Age' in the breed's development. He is a
successful breeder, exhibitor and judge, as well as Editor of the
prestigious American canine journal, *Kennel Review*.

## Veterinary consultant

Geoffrey J Cradock qualified at the Royal Veterinary College, London in
1947. He took over a veterinary practice in Surrey, where he concentrated
on developing the small animal side. He retired from the practice in 1983
to take a BA in Humanities at the Open University.
He now has a small-holding in Dorset where he pursues his principal
interest – dogs, birds, natural history and English literature.

## US consultant

Hal Sundstrom, as president of Halamar Inc, publishers of North Virginia,
has been editing and publishing magazines on travel and pure-bred dogs
since 1972. He is the recipient of six national writing and public excellence
awards from the Dog Writer's Association of America, of which he is now
president, and he is a past president of the Collie Club of America.
Hal has an extensive background and enormous experience in the dog
world as a breeder/handler/exhibitor, match and sweeps judge, officer
and director of specialty and all-breed clubs, show and symposium
chairman, and officer of the Arizona And Hawaii Councils of Dog Clubs.

# Introduction

I t was with great pleasure that I accepted the invitation to take part in this book on Cocker Spaniels. If my experiences over the last almost forty years can be of help, interest or guidance to anyone having their first puppy, breeding their first litter, or embarking on the exciting though sometimes disappointing world of showing, then I am glad to be able to share them with readers of this book.

I have had enormous happiness from my dogs – they ask so little and give so much. They have greatly enriched my life, not only through their companionship, but in meeting many people as a consequence of owning, breeding and showing Cockers. Travelling to other countries to judge has also enabled me to visit places of great interest and beauty, and I would not have spent my life in any other way.

## Responsibilities

For those who decide to devote more than a passing interest to dogs, one word of caution: engrossing though they are, try not to become oblivious to the many other activities and interests that life has to offer. If, however, your interest is purely as a pet

Left: *An experienced breeder of Cocker Spaniels is not only the best source of puppies, but will always be prepared to help and advise you on after-care.*

Above: *Frank Kane with his two American Cocker companions. Being handily-sized and adaptable, Cocker Spaniels will travel easily and happily in the car.*

owner, then I am sure you will benefit greatly from the love and companionship a Cocker Spaniel can offer. But please do not be tempted to buy a puppy before fully considering the responsibilities of ownership, ie you or someone trustworthy must be at home for the greater part of the day to feed, care for and train a new puppy; you must have access to adequate exercising areas; and make sure everyone in the household is as keen to own a dog as you are.

**Breeders**

It is important to seek out the best possible source of supply when you decide to buy a puppy. An experienced breeder is by far the best source; he or she will have years of experience in the breed, will know the virtues and disadvantages of the breed and will be able to guide you in the choice of the most suitable type and temperament for you and your family circumstances. Above all, they will be willing to help after you have taken delivery of your puppy. Do not hesitate to contact the breeder should you have any problems; to you they may seem enormous, but in fact may be quite routine to the breeder.

## Section One

# THE ENGLISH COCKER SPANIEL

# Chapter One

# A HISTORY OF THE ENGLISH COCKER SPANIEL

## SPANIEL ORIGINS

There are now several different varieties of Spaniel – the most popular and numerous being the Cocker. In 1892, the Cocker Spaniel was classified by the English Kennel Club as a separate breed; before Cockers were the smaller members of the Working Spaniel family.

Spaniels can trace their origins back several centuries, as exemplified by their depiction in paintings of the middle ages. The small Spaniel was many times depicted in paintings by Van Dyke, and other artists of that period.

The earliest mention of Spaniels in literature goes back many centuries, as far as the 12th century. Both Chaucer and his French contemporary, Gaston de Foix, write of a small sporting dog also well thought of as a companion. Both authors make mention of their working abilities, particularly in the bird hunting field.

In 1570, Dr Cains, Physician to

**Below:** *Ch Lily Obo. Owner, James Farrow of England, said: 'Lily was considered by most of our Spaniel experts to be the most typical Cocker ever exhibited.'*

Queen Elizabeth I, wrote in his book 'Englishe Dogges' of two breeds of Spaniels: a fowling dog, slightly larger in build, and a small 'Spaniell Gentle or Comfortor.' The word 'Comforter' meant, at that time, that any illness from which the owner was suffering would be transferred to the dog, if kept in close contact. At a later date, it was written that fleas or lice would also transfer from owner to dog.

King Charles II, of course, was famous as a great lover of the little Spaniels, and gave his name to the Cavalier. It is more than likely that they were one and the same.

It was not until the middle of the 19th century, when dog shows began to gain in popularity, that the division between the larger and smaller Spaniels began to take place. Spaniels over 25lbs (11kg) in weight were referred to as Field Spaniels, and those under the weight were called Cockers. It is also believed that Sussex Spaniels were involved at one stage during this transitional period.

It was about the year 1890 that the Kennel Club officially separated the varieties of Spaniel.

**The modern Cocker**
The modern Cocker, as it is today, is a result of selective breeding since the end of the last century.

Around the year 1880, the forerunner to the modern day English and American Cocker was born in England — his name was Obo. At that time, he was referred to as a Field Spaniel, and during his show career of approximately eight years, he was unbeaten. Champion Obo and his progeny were to feature in more than half the pedigrees of the next twenty years — both in the UK and the US.

Since that time, Cockers in both countries, have gone their separate ways, but without doubt both modern breeds originated from this one kennel belonging to Mr JJ Farrow. When the Cocker Spaniel Club was formed in England in 1902, Mr Farrow was one of the Founder Members together with, amongst others, Mr R Lloyd. He was the father of Mr HS Lloyd, who founded the 'of Ware' kennel. This world famous prefix is still playing an active part in the cocker spaniel breed to this day, in the hands of Mr Lloyd's daughter and granddaughter, Mrs Jennifer Carey and Paula Carey.

**Below:** *Ch Ted Obo, son of Ch Lily Obo, also owned by James Farrow, bred in 1987. His shorter body shows a progression towards the modern Cocker.*

Mr Lloyd, in collaboration with Mrs Jamieson Higgins of the Falconers Cockers, was an invincible force in the show world during the 1930s and up to World War II, 1939-45. The Falconers bitches were renowned for their lovely heads and correct type, and many went to found other kennels.

After World War II, many new lines began to appear to present challenges in the show ring. Perhaps one of the best known in parti-colours was Colinwood, whose Ch Colinwood Cowboy was the first postwar Champion. The Colinwoods were a formidable force from that time and during the next thirty years, with such famous winners as Ch Colinwood Silver Lariot (holder of many records in the breed); Sh Ch Colinwood Bunting; Sh Ch Colinwood Black Eagle, and the more recent Ch Colinwood Bellboy. Mr Collins' daughter, Mrs Phyllis Woolf is, as was her father, a recent Chairman of the Cocker Spaniel Club in the UK.

Many more famous lines have appeared in the last twenty years with great distinction: Thornfalcon, Crosbein, Bitcon, Bournehouse, Styvechale, Quaine, Peasemore, Okell, Craigleith, Matterhorn, Scolys, Weirdene, Lochdene, Classicway, Merryworth, Oxshott, Normanview, Cilleine, Tarling, etc.

In solid colours, the famous Broomleaf, Treetops, Lochranza, Sixshot and Misbourne strains made great strides just before and immediately after World War II. Many are still showing with great success up to the present day.

Other well known prefixes to appear with breeding and showing success include Kavora, Astrawin, Kenavon, Olanza, Canigou, Quettadene, Sorbrook and Helenwood, etc.

Several changes and improvements have been made to the Cocker over the years; in a comparison of photographs of the breed taken 50 years ago with those of the present day, several changes and improvements are apparent. The most notable improvement is that 'type' is much more level today. Coats have more feathering, backs are shorter, and the overall picture is of a more balanced animal.

**Below:** *Champion Fairholme Rally, a very famous show winner at the turn of the century. He was used extensively at stud and was responsible for many winners of his blue roan colouring.*

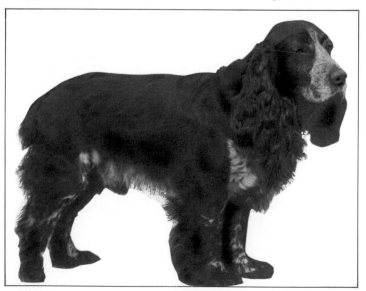

**Above:** *An engraving depicting Ch Obo with Ch Lily Obo, the forerunners of the breed as it is today. Obo was long in the back and low to the ground, which was the fashion of the 1880s.*

**Below:** *A group of Cocker Spaniel heads painted during the early part of the twentieth century. Each, in its own way, typifies the 'alert, eager to please' characteristic of the breed.*

# Chapter Two

# CHARACTERISTICS OF THE ENGLISH COCKER SPANIEL

The Cocker, since 1945, has become a great favourite with the dog-loving public as a companion for both town and country. The dog is of a compact size and of sturdy build, and providing it is exercised correctly, is at home in most surroundings. The Cocker's happy, lovable nature is without doubt its greatest asset, combined with a willingness to please and an enjoyment of most activities.

**In the field**

As a gundog, the Cocker has never lost its natural instinct to hunt and retrieve, even though the opportunities to work in the field are now fairly limited. There are still a few gundog societies which encourage their members to attend classes, held usually at the weekends, where it is possible to train a Cocker to a reasonably high standard in the field.

**Below:** *The Cocker Spaniel was originally used for flushing out game from dense cover. More recently it has taken on the role of all-round gundog.*

## In the ring

The Cocker is involved quite extensively in the show ring. Again, the breed's basic happy disposition makes it a good candidate for those of us who enjoy the thrill of the competitive life. More of this in the chapters on showing, pages 30-37 and 105-113.

## Family pet and companion

It is as a family companion that by far the greatest number of Cockers spend their lives. Their medium size enables them to be easily handled and to fit into the family car. As a house dog, the Cocker is glad to give warning of the approach of strangers and, if properly trained, will do just that. But this is not a dog to leave alone for long periods of time. I would not recommend having a Cocker if you are out at work all day; its inquisitive nature, particularly when young, can cause the dog and you a lot of trouble if it becomes bored.

The Cocker has an appealing head with long feathered ears, and as a puppy few breeds can surpass its attraction. But with the abundance of feathering in adult life, Cockers do require regular grooming and can be a liability to the busy town or city dweller on a wet day. However, if you put aside a short period of time each day to devote to its grooming, the Cocker's coat should not present too much of a problem (see the chapter on grooming, pages 23-25).

As a country dog, the Cocker is in its natural element. Anyone who has witnessed the ever-wagging tail of a Cocker loose in woods or fields will know that this is the result of instinctive traits; the ancestors of the modern Cocker were working, hunting dogs, and early writings and paintings confirm this.

**Below:** *Cocker puppies and kittens can become great friends, especially when they have grown up together in the home.*

# Chapter Three

# CHOOSING A PUPPY

**Above:** *This lovely family group shows a blue roan Cocker with her litter of four. Two resemble their mother in colour. The other two are blue roan and tan, offering the buyer a choice.*

**Right:** *Four of the many colours available: top left, orange roan; top right, blue roan and tan; bottom left, blue roan; bottom right, red or golden. Other colours are shown in the book.*

everal aspects have to be considered when choosing the right puppy for each individual owner.

**Sex**

The choice of male or female is usually one of the first considerations. This is a matter of personal preference, since there seems little evidence of a difference in temperament or intelligence between the sexes. It is thought that a dog can be slightly more difficult to house train, and if he is kept entire, he could roam and generally make a nuisance of himself when there are bitches in season in the neighbourhood. But this can be rectified by neutering. On the other hand, a bitch will need extra care during her twice-yearly seasons. Again, neutering (spaying) is the best answer to these 'seasonal' problems, if you do not plan to breed from your bitch, which is best carried out after her first season.

Thirty years ago, dog puppies were the most popular, but over the years the situation has changed to the reverse being the case now.

**Colours**

Cockers come in a large variety of very pretty colours: from all black

and all red or golden (the solid colours) to the parti-colours – blue roan; orange and chocolate roan; blue roan and tan; to clearly marked black and white; black, white and tan; orange and white; black and tan; and a few chocolate and tan. Your choice, again, is a matter of individual taste; all colours have their individual appeal.

### Buying your puppy

When you have decided on sex and colour, arrange a visit to a reputable breeder who specializes in your choice. You will find details of such breeders in the dog press – 'Our Dogs' or 'Dog World' in the UK; 'Dog World', 'Pure-Bred Dogs' and the 'American Kennel Gazette' in the US, the latter two publications being available by subscription from the American Kennel Club (address at the back of the book).

If you are looking for a puppy purely as a family pet, you can concentrate solely on choosing a healthy, happy, well-reared and attractive individual from a litter of Cockers at eight weeks old, without worrying unduly about the finer breed points. If, on the other hand, you are set on showing the dog at a later stage in its life, then there are more specific considerations in choosing a puppy – see the section on Choosing a Show Puppy, page 34, for practical advice.

Look for the liveliest puppy in the litter, rather than a quiet, shy one which might tempt you more, out of sympathy. The puppy should generally be ready to eat its food and play with its litter mates. Check the puppy's ears for odour or discharge – they should be clean and pink. Eyes should be bright; the mouth clean with white teeth. The puppy's coat should be glossy, and it should be 'well-covered' with flesh, ie neither too fat nor too thin.

Before taking your new puppy home, make sure you ask the breeder for a diet sheet, giving quantities, type of food and feeding times, which you should follow for the first few days at least. Ask the breeder for the dates when the puppy was wormed.

**Below:** *Having decided on colour and sex, the breeder will be happy to help you decide which puppy would be best suited to your family circumstances.*

# Chapter Four

# GROOMING YOUR ENGLISH COCKER SPANIEL

Cockers are a breed which needs regular grooming. If the 'feathering' is allowed to become too thick or matted, the ultimate solution is to have it all cut off and start again when it grows. If on the other hand a few minutes are spent each day in brushing the coat and furnishings on the ears and legs (when dry), this drastic action can be avoided.

**Brushing and combing the puppy**
Most breeders accustom their puppies from the age of four to five weeks to being groomed daily with a soft brush. Not only does this activity benefit the puppy, but it enables the breeder to inspect it for any sign of disorder, ie parasites or abrasions due to rough treatment from its litter mates. Its nails would have been periodically cut to protect its mother when feeding from her.

As soon as you take delivery of your puppy, start your grooming routine. It will only take about one minute for the first few weeks and is, at this stage, merely an exercise in disciplining the puppy and yourself into the habit. I would suggest that this is best undertaken in the morning, before the coat and feathering gets wet, if the weather is bad. In the early days, a soft brush and fine tooth comb with blunt teeth are all that is needed for a comb through and a gentle brushing. It is advisable to sit on the ground to gently brush the puppy. Start at the head doing each ear, down its neck, along its back, taking in both sides and finally down each leg, front and hind. The fine tooth comb is a necessity for removing any dead hair and parasites (see pages 78-79 for specific advice on dealing with parasites). If the grooming routine is swiftly followed by a tit-bit, such as a choc drop (doggy variety), it will be associated in the puppy's mind with a pleasurable experience.

**Changing of the coat**
Several changes occur in the dog's coat up to the time it reaches its first birthday. As a baby, its coat is short, shiny and almost devoid of feathering on its legs, ears and tummy. As it approaches six months of age, the feathering will begin to grow longer and thicker, and great care must be taken to keep it free from knots, as I have already stressed. The armpits are the most usual place for mats to appear; my own opinion is that the friction as the dog walks may be the cause. It is kinder to keep this area free from feathering if it continually mats up as not only is it a very sensitive place, but if wet it is uncomfortable for the dog.

If your choice of colour is black, your puppy will, in all probability, begin to grow a noticeable amount of feathering even as young as three to four months, particularly on its ears and front legs. Other colours are usually less heavily feathered on maturity and are consequently later growing their furnishings.

To keep the feathering free from knots and mats, the addition of a slicker and a wide-toothed comb to your basic equipment will be necessary, as well as a stiffer brush for the ears and leg feathering. If, however, you choose to have a golden or a parti-colour Cocker, your grooming task should be easier, although some of these colours carry heavier coats than others. I have seen sparsely coated blacks, but in general, the above remarks apply.

Remember to wash all grooming equipment once a week.

### Trimming

If you decide to leave the actual trimming to a professional, then ask the breeder to recommend someone who will take on the job of trimming your Cocker. Quite a few breeders will do some trimming themselves, so you may not need to look any further. It is a good idea to have the feet, and perhaps under the ears and chin tidied up at about four months. This not only reduces the amount of grit and dirt brought in to the house after exercise, but it educates the puppy to being trimmed as an adult. Try to stay with the dog for the first trim to give it confidence. After that, the dog will probably become used to these trips to the hairdresser.

If, however, you decide to invest in some equipment to do the trimming yourself, then ask the breeder, or someone used to trimming Cockers, to show you how to do it properly. It is not an art that can be learnt overnight, so prepare for mistakes, and hours of practice. The chapter on showing in this section of the book (pages 35-37) gives basic instructions and accompanying photographs for preparing your Cocker for the show ring, including trimming, which you can follow for your pet Cocker.

### Bathing

Frequent bathing is not necessary for the Cocker which is regularly groomed with a brush. However, if the dog goes for a swim in dirty water, or rolls in dirt, it will be necessary to bath it in order to make it liveable with (see pages 54-55 for practical advice on bathing).

There are many good insecticidal shampoos available, or you can use a human shampoo. Do make sure the dog is well and truly dry before it is bedded down for the night. Dry shampoos, either powder, foam or spirit, will freshen the Cocker up should you want it to look its best for any special reason.

---

**Below:** *It is preferable to use thinning scissors to shorten the ear feathering on the pet Cocker since this is a particularly sensitive part of the body.*

**Above:** *A wide-toothed comb should be used daily to keep the ear feathering free from knots and mats. Shortening of the feathering makes the task easier.*

**Below:** *The use of a slicker brush will help to remove dead hair from the body coat and feathering, and can be used to remove puppy coat when ready.*

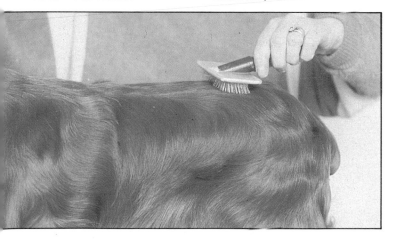

# Chapter Five

# BREEDING: HEREDITARY PROBLEMS

The majority of pet Cocker owners are not interested in this aspect, but there will always be a few, like myself, who having bought a puppy and read a few books on the breed, decide to go one step further and let their beloved pet bitch have a litter. With hindsight, I think as far as I am concerned, I would still be of the same mind were it all to be happening today. But it requires a lot of thought before embarking on such a serious undertaking. Not only is it a tremendous responsibility and very hard work, it can also be a very expensive exercise. It needs 24-hour vigilance during the first week or so after the babies have arrived. Most Cocker bitches are easy whelpers, but as with any animal there are the exceptions, and a good relationship with your veterinarian, who would like to be informed of the whelping in advance, is essential.

## Hereditary problems

These must be seriously considered before breeding from any bitch. The list of hereditary problems associated with the Cocker Spaniel may seem somewhat daunting at first sight, but it must be remembered that such a list can be compiled for any breed of dog, and the majority of Cocker Spaniels do not suffer from any of these recorded problems.

When breeding your first litter, ask the advice of an experienced breeder. He or she will be aware of the lines that carry the possibility of producing cases of hereditary disease, and will not advise the doubling up of certain blood lines. There will always be the possibility of unexpected things, both good

and bad, turning up in any litter, and the art of breeding is to avoid this happening if at all possible. If, however careful you are in choosing a mate for your bitch, your litter suffers from any of the following problems, then on no account repeat the mating, or that of close relatives.

**Hereditary Cataract (HC)** Cataracts can develop quite early in a dog's life, from about one year old, or they can develop much later. They may be present in one or both eyes, and they can cause partial or total blindness.

Controversy has raged over the mode of inheritance of hereditary cataract. General opinion now seems agreed that the condition is inherited as a recessive trait, which makes the problem that much more difficult since there is the added complication of carrier animals. A carrier is an animal which is not clinically afflicted with the disease, but carries the chromosome for that disease, and is therefore capable of passing on the disease when mated to another carrier. Hence, it is possible for two clinically clear (unaffected) animals to produce a percentage of affected offspring. It is impossible to clinically detect a carrier but it must be born in mind that both parents of an affected animal must themselves be affected or be carriers.

There are six possible combinations of mating, based on the supposition that each parent can be either affected, unaffected or a

**Below:** *A veterinarian using an opthalmosocope to examine the eyes for any sign of hereditary eye diseases, including Hereditary Cataract, Progressive Retinal Atrophy and Entropion. Do not breed from affected animals.*

carrier. The resulting litters, will, on average be as follows:

**1** Both parents affected – all progeny affected.
**2** One parent affected, one carrier parent – 50% affected, 50% carriers.
**3** One parent affected, one parent free – all progeny carriers.
**4** Both parents carriers – 50% carriers, 25% free, 25% affected.
**5** One parent free, one carrier parent – 50% carriers, 50% free.
**6** Both parents free – all progeny free.

Such findings have serious implications for those interested in breeding Cockers including the American Cocker (see pages 56-57). It would be immoral to breed from any afflicted animal and unwise to use an animal which had an afflicted litter mate. Do not use for breeding a son or daughter of an afflicted animal. Remember also that if a dog or bitch has produced an afflicted puppy then it follows that both parents of that puppy **must** be carriers. There is an element of risk therefore in all matings.

Another complication in preventing and avoiding this condition is the fact that, in some cases, HC is not detected until middle age or later and by this time the dog has been bred from, thus perpetuating the problem. One can deduce from this some good, general advice for breeding: do not breed from very young stock. Avoid breeding if possible from stock until it is three years old, by which time HC might have arisen. Older dogs who have not developed the condition themselves and who have not produced any affected offspring are the safest breeding stock, and worth their weight in gold to the serious breeder.

## Progressive Retinal Atrophy (PRA)
PRA is first diagnosed when the dog has difficulty seeing in the dark ('night blindness'), and from this first stage there is a gradual degeneration of the retina leading to total blindness.

It is generally agreed that PRA is inherited through a recessive gene, therefore, following the same pattern of inheritance as hereditary cataract. The same advice on the latter regarding diagnosis and breeding principles applies. It is possible to diagnose quite early on in life whether a dog will develop PRA. This is possible with the advanced veterinary technology – using an electro retinagram, thus minimising the risk of breeding from stock which will later go down with the disease.

**Entropion** This is a turning in of the eyelids, causing irritation to the eye. In most cases, surgery is successful. Do not breed from affected dogs.

**Hip dysplasia** This is an abnormality of the hip joint or joints. It can be found on one side only, or both. The degree of lameness depends on the severity of the disease. Mildly affected cases do not exhibit any clinical signs. The inheritance pattern is multi-factorial and therefore difficult to access.

**Slipping patellas (Patella luxation)** This condition can affect one or both hind legs. It is caused by the ligaments which hold the knee

cap (patella) in place being weak, thus allowing the patella to slip from its normal position. It can be painful, but not always.

**Uncertain temperament** Recent studies have indicated that this has no hereditary pattern, but personally I would not breed from a dog with a temperamental fault, particularly if of an aggressive nature. Early upbringing can cause defects in behaviour patterns.

**Familial nephropathy (Shrunken kidneys)** This has been the subject of recent veterinary study, both clinically and genetically. It is thought to be caused by a recessive gene. Therefore, to produce a case, both parents must be assumed to be carriers of the disease. Symptoms are noticed usually at 6-12 months of age, but have been observed in younger or older puppies. Urine tests are available to diagnose. Signs are loss of weight, excessive thirst, and a reluctance to eat, resulting in general malaise. Carriers should not be bred from unless on veterinary advice, ie test mating.

**Affected puppies**
Over the years, the breed clubs have endeavoured to tackle these

**Above:** *A litter of black and white puppies outwardly almost identical, but their individual genetic makeup will determine the colour of their offspring.*

hereditary conditions before they become 'epidemic'. Alas, the breeding world is no more perfect than the world in general. Some irresponsible 'get rich quick' commercial breeders have paid little attention to the knowledge available since these studies have taken place, and have continued to breed from affected stock. This has spread the trouble that much further.

Should you be unfortunate in acquiring a puppy which has one of these defects, then the first person to contact is the breeder. It may well be that he or she is oblivious to the fact that his or her stock is affected. But it is important to tell the breeder so that he or she can avoid a recurrence by repeating the mating of the affected puppies' parents.

It is quite possible that the breeder will feel he or she wants to compensate in one of two ways. He or she may suggest replacing the puppy, or may offer to pay, either in part or full, for any operation or treatment given to improve the condition of the affected dog.

# Chapter Six

# SHOWING YOUR ENGLISH COCKER SPANIEL

Every breed of dog has its own standard of points, which the judge applies to every dog when assessing a class in the show ring. The winner is the dog which, in the judge's opinion, measures up most closely to that standard. The standard details the physical features that are desirable and which constitute a typical example of the breed.

## The UK Breed Standard

The specialist breed clubs in Australia also use the UK Kennel Club Breed Standards.

**General appearance**   Merry, sturdy, sporting; well balanced; compact; measuring approximately same from withers to ground as from withers to root of tail.

**Characteristics**   Merry nature with every-wagging tail, shows a typical bustling movement, particularly when following scent, fearless of heavy cover.

**Temperament**   Gentle and affectionate, yet full of life and exuberance.

**Head and skull**   Square muzzle, with distinct stop set midway between tip of nose and occiput. Skull well developed, cleanly chiselled, neither too fine nor too coarse. Cheek bones not prominent. Nose sufficiently wide for acute scenting power.

**Eyes**   Full, but not prominent. Dark brown or brown, never light, but in the case of liver, liver roan, and liver and white, dark hazel to harmonise with coat; with expression of intelligence and gentleness but wide awake, bright and merry; rims tight.

**Ears**   Lobular, set low on a level with eyes. Fine leathers extending to nose tip. Well clothed with long straight silky hair.

**Mouth**   Jaws strong with a perfect, regular scissor bite, ie upper teeth closely overlapping the lower teeth and set square to the jaws.

**Neck**   Moderate in length, muscular. Set neatly into fine sloping shoulders. The throat should be clean.

**Forequarters**   Shoulders sloping and fine. Legs well boned, straight, sufficiently short for concentrated power. Not too short to interface with tremendous exertions expected from this grand, sporting dog.

**Body**   Strong, compact. Chest well developed and brisket deep; neither too wide nor too narrow in front. Ribs well sprung. Loin short, wide with firm, level topline gently sloping downwards to tail from end of loin to set on of tail.

**Hindquarters**   Wide, well rounded, very muscular. Legs well boned, good bend of stifle, short below hock allowing for plenty of drive.

**Feet**   Firm, thickly padded, cat-like.

**Tail**   Set on slightly lower than line of back. Must be merry in action and carried level, never cocked up. Customarily docked but never too short to hide, nor too long to interfere with the incessant merry action when working.

**Gait/movement** True through action with great drive covering ground well.

**Coat** Flat, silky in texture, never wiry or wavy, not too profuse and never curly. Well feathered forelegs, body and hindlegs above hocks.

**Colour** Various. In self colours no white allowed except on chest.

**Size** Height approximately: Dogs 39-41cm (15½-16in); bitches 38-39cm (15-15½in). Weight approximately 28-32lbs (13-14.5kg).

**Faults** Any departure from the foregoing points should be considered a fault and the seriousness with which the fault should be regarded should be in exact proportion to its degree.

**Note** Male animals should have two apparently normal testicles fully descended into the scrotum.

**The US Breed Standard**
**General appearance** The English Cocker Spaniel is an attractive, active, merry sporting dog; with short body and strong limbs,

**Skeleton**
*1 Mandible 2 Maxilla 3 Eye socket 4 Skull 5 Atlas 6 Axis 7 Cervical vertebrae 8 Scapula (shoulder blade) 9 Thoracic vertebrae 10 Ribs 11 Lumber vertebrae 12 Pelvis 13 Coccygeal vertebrae 14 Phalanges 15 Fibula 16 Tibia 17 Metatarsals 18 Patella 19 Ulna 20 Humerus 21 Radius*

**Conformation points**
A Muzzle B Foreface C Stop D Cheek E Occiupt F Neck G Shoulder H Withers I Back J Loin K Stifle or knee L Stern M Hock N Feathering O chest P Forearm Q Pastern R Brisket

The diagram is based on the Kennel Club Standard (UK), approved 1969.

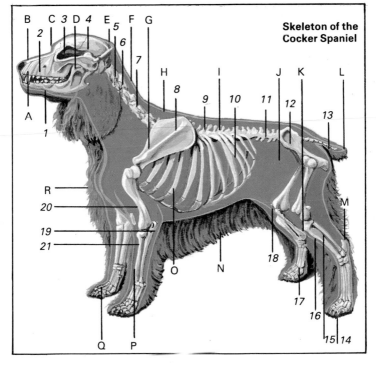

**Skeleton of the Cocker Spaniel**

standing well up at the withers. His movements are alive with energy; his gait powerful and frictionless. He is alert at all times, and the carriage of head and incessant action of his tail while at work give the impression that here is a dog that is not only bred for hunting, but really enjoys it. He is well balanced, strongly built, full of quality and is capable of top speed combined with great stamina. His head imparts an individual stamp peculiar to him alone and has that brainy appearance expressive of the highest intelligence; and is in perfect proportion to his body. His muzzle is a most distinctive feature, being of correct conformation and in proportion to his skull.

**Character** The character of the English Cocker is of extreme importance. His love and faithfulness to his master and household, his alertness and courage are characteristic. He is noted for his intelligence and merry disposition; not quarrelsome; and is a responsive and willing worker both in the field and as a companion.

**Head** The skull and forehead should be well developed with no suggestion of coarseness, arched and slightly flattened on top when viewed both from the stop to the end of the skull as well as from ear to ear, and cleanly chiselled under the eyes. The proportion of the head desirable is approximately one half for the muzzle and one half for the skull. The muzzle should be square with a definite stop where it blends into the skull and in proportion with the width of the skull. As the English Cocker is primarily a sporting dog, the muzzle and jaws must be of sufficient strength and size to carry game; and the length of the muzzle should provide room for the development of the olfactory nerve to insure good scenting qualities, which require that the nose be wide and well developed. Nostrils black in colour except in reds, livers, parti-colours and roans of the lighter shades, where brown is permissible, but black preferred. Lips should be square, full and free from flews. Teeth should be even

and set squarely. *Faults* Muzzle too short and snipy. Jaw overshot or undershot. Lips snipy or pendulous. Skull too flat or too rounded, cheeky or coarse. Stop insufficient or exaggerated.

**Eyes** The eyes should be of medium size, full and slightly oval shaped; set squarely in skull and wide apart. Eyes must be dark brown except in livers and light parti-colours where hazel is permissible, but the darker the better. The general expression should be intelligent, alert, bright and merry. *Faults* Light, round or protruding eyes. Conspicuous haw.

**Ears** Lobular; set low and close to the head; leather fine and extending at least to the nose, well covered with long, silky straight or slightly wavy hair. *Faults* Set or carried too high; too wide at the top; insufficient feathering; positive curls or ringlets.

**Neck** Long, clean and muscular; arched towards the head; set cleanly into sloping shoulders. *Faults* Short; thick; with dewlap or excessive throatiness.

**Body** Close coupled, compact and firmly knit, giving the impression of great strength without heaviness. Depth of brisket should reach to the elbow, sloping gradually upward to the loins. Ribs should spring gradually to middle of body, tapering to back ribs which should be of good depth and extend well back. *Faults* Too long and lacking depth; insufficient spring of rib; barrel rib.

**Shoulders and chest** Shoulders sloping and fine; chest deep and well developed but not too wide and round to interfere with the free action of the forelegs. *Faults* Straight or loaded shoulders.

**Back and loin** Back short and strong. Length of back from withers to tail-set should be approximate height from ground to withers. Height of the dog at the withers should be greater than the height at the hip joint, providing a gradual slope between these points. Loin short and powerful, slightly arched. *Faults* Too low at withers; long, sway-back or roach back; flat or

narrow loin; exaggerated tuck-up.

**Forelegs** Straight and strong with bone nearly equal in size from elbow to heel; elbows set close to the body with free action from shoulders; pasterns short, straight and strong. *Faults* Shoulders loose; elbows turned in or out; legs bowed or set too close or too wide apart; knees knuckled over; light bone.

**Feet** Size in proportion to the legs; firm, round and catlike with thick pads and strong toes. *Faults* Too large, too small; spreading or splayed.

**Hindquarters** The hips should be rounded; thighs broad; well developed and muscular, giving abundance of propelling power. Stifles strong and well bent. Hock to pad moderately short, strong and well let down. *Faults* Excessive angulation; lightness of bone; stifle too short; hocks too long or turned in or out.

**Tail** Set on to conform with the topline of the back. Merry in action. *Faults* Set too low; habitually carried too high; too short or too long.

**Colour** Various. In self colours a white shirt frill is undesirable. In parti-colours, the colouring must be broken on the body and be evenly distributed. No large portion of any one colour should exist. White should be shown on the saddle. A

**Above:** *Sh Ch Canigou Mr Happy, Cocker of the Year, 1986 in the UK. He illustrates superbly the desired characteristics.*

dog of any solid colour with white feet and chest is not a parti-colour. In roans it is desirable that the white hair should be distributed over the body, the more evenly the better. Roans come in various colours: blue, liver, red, orange and lemon. In black and tans the coat should be black; tan spots over the eyes, tan on the sides of the muzzle, on the throat and chest, on forelegs from the knees to the toes and on the hind legs on the inside of the legs, also on the stifle and extending back from the hock to the toes. .

*Faults* White feet are undesirable in any specimen of self colour.

**Coat** On head, short and fine; on body, flat or slightly wavy and silky in texture. Should be of medium length with enough undercoating to give protection. The English Cocker should be well feathered but not so profusely as to hide the true lines or interfere with his field work.

*Faults* Lack of coat; too soft, curly or wiry. Excessive trimming to change the natural appearance and coat should be discouraged.

**Height** Ideal heights at withers: Males, 16-17in (40.5-43cm); females, 15-16in (38-40.5cm).

Deviations to be severely penalized but not disqualified.

**Weight**  The most desirable weights: Males, 28-34lbs (13-15.5kg); females, 26-32lbs (12-14.5kg). Proper physical conformation and balance should be considered more important than weight alone.

## CHOOSING A SHOW PUPPY

Even the most experienced of breeders find it impossible to be sure how an eight-week old puppy will look as an adult; all one can say is that he or she shows early promise of growing in to a worthy representative of the breed. If you are sure you want a show specimen, it is advisable to buy a Cocker of at least nine months of age. By this age, the dog should have reached its adult size and cut its second teeth. It will also be possible to see how the dog is developing both in coat, movement and temperament. The older puppy will, of course, cost more – it will have been vaccinated, trained, reared and generally looked after for six to seven months by its breeder, and all this is time and money consuming.

The puppy should stand over its quarters and have a good bend of stifle, but not in any way exaggerated. The head should be balanced, ie the skull and foreface should be approximately of the same width. The stop and eye placement should be at the halfway mark. Eyes should be neither small nor large, and give a 'soft' look so important to the correct expression (see the Breed Standard for more detail). The tail should not be carried higher than the back; puppies often exhibit high tail carriage due to over exuberance and excitability. Check the parents if possible – if they are correct in this point, then in all probability the puppy will be too.

The standard of breeding is excellent nowadays, and if you go to a reliable source you will no doubt find yourself the proud owner of a typical Cocker.

**Below:** *A beautiful golden puppy showing the ideal sweet eye and expression; well-defined stop; balance of skull and muzzle.*

**Below right:** *Removing surplus hair by the finger and thumb method; a technique aided by the use of chalk or finger stalls.*

## SHOW GROOMING

Preparing a coat for the show ring is a long-term exercise. So many factors come in to play when one is aiming at the highest level of preparation needed. Exercise is important – it firms the muscles, increases the blood supply to the skin, thereby encouraging the coat to grow to its maximum. Feeding is also important to help nourish the animal, also reflected in the condition of the Cocker's coat.

The Standard calls for a flat, silky textured coat, with feathering on ears, legs and tummy. Much depends on the type of natural coat your dog is blessed with. If it has a very flat, sparse coat, the dog may be short of feathering. On the other hand, if its body coat is fairly thick, its feathering will most likely be of a generous proportion also. If you have already brushed and combed your dog daily, as recommended in the chapter on grooming (pages 23-25), then your task will be much easier, whatever the type of coat.

### Trimming the puppy
Let us assume, then, that your puppy is knot-free, and that its puppy 'fluff' is coming out daily in the brush and comb. By far the best method of removing surplus hair and excess puppy coat is by the finger and thumb method. When you become proficient at this, it will not hurt your dog at all.

It is a mistake to remove a puppy coat before it is loose enough to come out easily. It will either break off halfway along the hair shaft, or you will find yourself with a coat that looks 'moth-eaten', with many bald patches. It takes several months for a coat to grow back if removed in this way, so do be patient and wait for it to come out naturally and easily. Cocker puppies look attractive in their natural fluffy coats up to the age of nine to ten months; the judges do not expect them to have an adult coat at this stage. However, it **is** expected for them to have their feet trimmed, and the excess hair removed from the top of head, ears and hocks.

### Trimming the adult
The aim is for short hair on the top of the head. Remove any long 'top-knot' by pulling out gradually, and also the tufty hair which grows at the junction of the ears and skull. It is also desirable to clean out the

stop (the space between the eyes), and also any hair growing on the foreface and sides of the nose. Under no circumstances try to pull your dog's whiskers out – it is very painful, and you may alienate your dog for a long time. A sharp pair of scissors will cut the whiskers close to the short facial hair, without them looking obviously cut.

There are some areas where it is neither necessary nor desirable – owing to the skin being very tender – to pull out the hair. These are the back of and under the ears, under the chin and down the throat. The use of thinning scissors on these parts gives a satisfactory result. In order to define the back of the skull and enhance the length of the neck, pull the excess hair from this region until there is a gentle indentation at the base of the skull. Continue pulling the hair down the back of the neck and gradually on to the shoulders. It is better to leave the hair longer from here right down the back until the region where the tail begins. At this point, a mixture of pulling and use of the thinning scissors can be employed. A neat tail with a small amount of hair at the end looks better than one that is severely barbered.

The hair under the tail will need thinning and tidying to enable the hair to lie as flat as possible under the tail. The hocks are another area

**Above:** *Front view of two blue roans – the left has been show groomed by a combination of hand stripping and scissor-thinning.*

where use of the thinning scissors is possible. Do not trim the hair too close; a thick, tidy look is the aim.

Trimming of the feet both front and back are a skill not easily learned. The aim is to achieve a cat-like appearance, and the ease or difficulty of your task depends on how correct the feet are to begin with. A thin, flat foot can be improved by leaving the hair thicker on the top of the foot just behind the nails, and taking the side hair very close to the foot. If the feet are good, then the hair should be shortened all round to give the neatest appearance possible.

The next areas to be tidied are the sides of the rib cage, where the tummy feathering grows long. Quite often, short tufty hair grows here and is best removed by pulling to give a tidy, flat side.

To achieve the overall, desired finish, will take time; it is better to tackle a part of a portion of the body at each session, rather than try to finish say the head, or the body completely before starting the next part. Allow yourself plenty of time so that, in this way, you should complete the preparation of the dog gradually, and will not have to do a rush job on any one area when the show day draws near.

## Bathing and drying

About three days before the show, most dogs benefit from a bath. I say most, as there are a few dogs who do not seem to need a bath each time. The method of drying the coat is all important.

There are several satisfactory ways of drying the coat, and the method chosen will determine the result. The most effective procedure is described in detail on page 55, as applied to the American Cocker.

## Making the best of your dog

No dog is perfect, and in a breed which is trimmed, it is possible to enhance the weaker points by careful trimming. For instance, if the dog is short of neck, you will want to take as much hair away as possible. If it has a slightly long back, then the removal of as much hair on the chest and under the tail will tend to make the dog look shorter in back.

A coarse skull will need careful cleaning out, particularly at the top of the ears. Too short or too long a tail can be improved by careful trimming.

None of these suggestions are meant to convey the notion that you will fool the experienced judge. He, or she, will use his or her hands to judge your dog, and experience will tell him or her of the true confor-mation of the animal. But it is quite in order to make the best of your dog's good points, and minimise its faults.

**Below:** *Comparative rear views of the same Cockers – the right before show preparation, the left correctly show-groomed.*

# Section Two

# THE AMERICAN COCKER SPANIEL

# Chapter One

# A HISTORY OF THE AMERICAN COCKER SPANIEL

**Foundation of Cockers in the US**

Both the American Cocker Spaniel and the English Cocker Spaniel descend from the same stock. The acknowledged foundation of both breeds is the black Cocker Spaniel, Ch Obo, whelped in England in June 1879. He was the offspring of a Sussex Spaniel sire and a Field Spaniel dam, yet eligible for English Stud Book registry as a Cocker Spaniel. The regulations of a Spaniel in the Stud Book in England as a 'Cocker Spaniel' did not mean its sire, dam, or any of its ancestors were registered as 'Cocker Spaniels'.

In those days it was in order for breeders of sporting Spaniels to register puppies from a Spaniel litter as being of different strains, varieties or breeds, according to what use the breeder thought the pup might adapt to in the field. There was no consideration given to the puppy's background or ancestry.

Needless-to-say, disappointments and confusion often resulted from breedings made to English registered Cockers. This primarily was due to the Americans lacking an understanding of the English system of classifying for stud book registration purposes.

Returning to Ch Obo. It appears Obo was long of back and very low to the ground, which was the accepted fashion of the day. However, his get won well at all the English shows and a number of

them were exported to America. At the end of the nineteenth century, that stock became the foundation for Cockers in North America.

Chloe II was imported in whelp to Ch Obo. She whelped a litter in the United States containing Obo II, American Kennel Club No 4911. It appears Obo II was somewhat of a step forward in that he was described as follows: 'A compactly built little fellow. His head a little strong but it is nicely carried; his coat is dense and flat and his legs and feet first class.'

Other descriptions showed him to be a very 'sporting type of dog but not without faults; skull showing slight coarseness. Muzzle should be deeper, with a cleaner cut appearance in every direction; it is wider than we like and the lower incisors project slightly'. In the end, however, Obo II was generally considered 'The Prince of Stud Dogs' and was accepted as the 'Model Cocker' by the American fancy. By 1920, there were few if any Cockers in America which did not have Obo II blood coursing through their veins.

Robinhurst Foreglow was one of his descendants whelped in 1961. He was a descendent of Obo's on both sides. Evidently, he had not only inherited his illustrious predecessor's many qualities but ensuring generations had corrected many of the faults as well. Foreglow was also heavily bred as he was considered a 'thoroughly modern type Cocker', well up on the leg, more robust in every way and bold and fearless as well. He gave the fancy a much clearer picture of what it wanted.

The next major step seemed to be Ch Torohill Trader, a Foreglow descendent whom he closely resembled. Trader, however, was black while Foreglow was red. The two dogs were very much the same type but Trader was to bring the breed an exceptional headpiece and expression.

### Evolution of two types

While the British breeders carried on with the type of Cocker they favoured, in America an interesting (and confusing) situation was developing. The Cocker was evolving into two 'types' – American and English; each with loyal supporters, but the English devotees far fewer in number.

Selective breeding was again in progress and what had developed a recognizable 'Cocker' at the turn of the century was developing an 'American' Cocker in the late 1920s and early 1930s. It must be kept in mind though that the American Kennel Club still registered all as 'Cocker Spaniels' whether imported, native or a blend.

At this time, while both types were very much more 'up on leg' than those of the 'Obo' era, distinct differences were readily apparent. The main one being in head type.

Those favouring the English type feared it would be lost forever and in 1936 formed the English Cocker Spaniel Club of America. The members of that organization pledged not to interbreed the two varieties. It must be remembered though that there were still many breeders of the English type who neither knew of the club's goals nor cared and continued to interbreed and register with the AKC, which made no distinction itself. But the stalwart members of the ECSCA worked to make the English Cocker legitimate in the eyes of the AKC. This necessitated a tremendous pedigree purge allowing only those dogs with five generations of pure English breeding to be identified as 'pure English Cockers'.

---

**Below:** *An early black and tan Cocker Spaniel, which played a part in the development of the American Cocker type. It was called Robinhurst Wary, owned by the Honourable Townsend Scudder.*

## Separate breed status

In September 1946, the goals of the ECSCA were realized when the AKC granted separate breed status to the two 'types': English and Americans with three distinct varieties (Black, ASCOB and Parti-colour) being recognized of the latter.

The American type breeders strove to develop their breed into a shorter-backed, shorter-headed, higher-domed, up-on-leg and heavier coated animal. That is, basically, the prototype of the American Cocker as we know it today.

Down from Torohill Trader came a succession of better dogs and direction-taking sires. Among them Ch Stockdlae Startler, Ch Try Cob's Candidate and on down to Ch Stockdale Town Talk, Ch Myroy Night Rocket and Rocket's son (who was to become the cornerstone of the modern black in America), Ch Elderwood Bangaway.

## The Blacks and Black and Tans

Bangaway must be acknowledged by all serious students of the breed as the typesetter for the Black and Black and Tan Cocker of today. He was whelped in 1950. His son, Ch De Karlo's Dashaway and grandsons, Ch Valli-Lo's Flashaway and Ch Clarkdale Capitol Stock, stand behind practically every known producing and winning line of Black and Black and Tan American Cockers in America today.

## Parti-colours and Buffs

While the Parti-colour and Buffs descended from the same stock as their Black cousins, their development was slower. However, it was none-the-less abrupt and dramatic.

Bea Weygeson of the famed Honey Creek Parti-colours singlehandedly developed a line resplendent in coat, markings, head and expression. They took the variety by storm in the late 1940s. She took the blood of Ch Bobb's Master Showman and through a series as astute line and inbreedings, developed the foundation for today's Parti-colour. Honeycreek,

**Above:** *A study of Red Brucie, who was a son of Robinhurst Foreglow. He was a most influential sire in the 1920s in the evolution of the American Cocker Spaniel.*

together with advantageous solid crosses, is responsible for the variety as we see it today.

The Buffs were the last of the three varieties to step forward into the limelight by becoming competitive in coat and glamour. While it was accomplished almost entirely in the 1950s through the influence of Ch Maddies Vagabonds Return and his son, Ch Gravel Hill Gold Opportunity, credit must be given to the existing Eash's Golden Boy-Biggs' Cover Charge line, with which the two dogs nicked so well.

Return and Gold Opportunity also contributed heavily to the Parti Variety. While excelling in beauty, the Parti-colour variety suffered from some unsoundness physically and temperamentally. Parti breeders desperately needed an outcross. Vagabonds Return and Gold Opportunity provided that outcross and their blood, added to that of Honeycreek, combined to produce the modern day pillar of the Parti variety, the famous Ch Scioto Bluff Sinbad.

**Above:** *A fine example of today's buffs. Although this colour was late in being developed, it is now very popular both in the show ring and as a family pet.*

So, while the groundwork for today's American Cocker spanned several decades, the most significant developments occurred in the late 1940s and early '50s, referred to by many as the 'Golden Age' of the American Cocker Spaniel. What had been conceived was achieved in that era. What followed has been variations on a theme.

### Recent developments
A relatively 'modern' breed, the American Cocker is still evolving and developing, the breed standard being revised by the AKC in 1973.

There has been a gradual increase in the amount of coat on the American Cocker, and although some judges penalise a coat which is too profuse and although the average owner might find such profusion impractical, it is still regarded as the crowning glory of the breed and it would be almost impossible to win in the show ring today with a sparsely coated specimen.

The American Cocker has remained for the past forty years one of the ten most popular breeds in its homeland, whilst its beauty, temperament and showmanship have attracted a growing band of foreign devotees, leading to the exportation and establishment of the breed in many countries of the World.

### Introduction into the UK
The American Cocker was introduced into the UK as recently as the early 1960s, via an importation of a bitch from Holland. Various imports from the States added new bloodlines and the breed became established. Many established kennels in other breeds took an interest in this breed which quickly grew and by 1968 sufficient Kennel Club Registrations enabled the breed to qualify for its first allocation of KC Challenge Certifications, to progress from the Any Variety Not Separately Classified to its own breed classification.

Although the American Cocker has remained a popular show dog in the UK and gained some popularity as a household pet, it has not reduced the much greater popularity of its English counterpart, which remains high on the list of favourite breeds in the UK.

# Chapter Two

# CHARACTERISTICS OF THE AMERICAN COCKER SPANIEL

The American Cocker is one of the most glamorous and beautiful breeds of dog. Its beautiful head, appealing eyes and luxuriantly-coated legs and body make it a real eyecatcher. The dog's jaunty, purposeful movement indicates its sporting and fun-loving nature. Temperament-wise, the American Cocker is a joy to own: happy, affectionate, always eager to please and ever faithful. Aggressiveness and treachery are extreme rarities, and this lovely temperament is what recommends the breed so strongly as a pet.

### Sporting dog or family companion

Handily sized, intelligent and quick to learn, the American Cocker is adaptable to both town and country life. As a sporting dog, it is always ready for exercise, but it enjoys too the comforts of family life at home.

As a family pet and companion, the American Cocker is a real winner: ask someone who owns one (Yanks as they are popularly called in the UK) and they will tell you that they would not be without one. The American Cocker is not, thankfully, one of the more commercial breeds of pedigree dogs, but amongst those who know the breed, it inspires a special loyalty and affection. The American Cocker is a real personality dog!

### Colours

The American Cocker comes in a range of attractive colours: black, all shades of buff, gold and red,

*Below: This energetic American Cocker takes full advantage of open country down by the sea.*

chocolate, black and tan; and the parti-colours: black and white, red and white, tri-colour, chocolate and white.

## Important considerations

Whilst the American's abundant coat is its crowning glory, it must be pointed out that it demands, of necessity, a great amount of grooming and care to keep it in order. The responsible owner must undertake to groom his or her dog regularly, to have it trimmed periodically – or learn to trim the dog him or herself. The American Cocker is also, like many other breeds, smitten with some hereditary problems, principally that of hereditary cataract, which, if it arises, can cause partial or complete blindness. It must be pointed out here, however, that responsible breeders are doing their utmost to eradicate the problem and thus minimise the possibility of breeding puppies which will develop this condition. Further discussion on this, and other hereditary problems, will be found in Chapter Five on pages 56 to 57.

## In the ring

As a show dog, the American Cocker is a 'natural'. There are few more beautiful sights than a well presented, full coated American sailing round the ring with the drive and style which are such features of the breed.

**Below:** *Some attractive American Cocker colours; top row – buff and black; bottom row – black and white and black and tan.*

# Chapter Three

# CHOOSING A PUPPY

## Where to buy

Having decided that you can cope with the responsibilities of owning a dog, and having decided that the American Cocker is the breed for you, the problem then arises of finding a suitable puppy. It is important to buy a puppy from a reputable breeder of American Cockers.

A visit to a local dog show might bring you into contact with a breeder, or, by asking other Spaniel exhibitors at the show, you might be given a breeder's name and address. Do not expect the first breeder with whom you make contact to have puppies available at that precise moment. You may have to wait several months for a puppy, or the breeder may refer you to someone else further afield who may have stock available.

## Questions for the breeder

Before buying an American Cocker puppy from any breeder, there are several questions which you, the buyer, **must** ask. They are questions which no responsible breeder will mind answering.

Of crucial importance is the eye condition of the parents. Ask to see the eye certificates (certified by a veterinarian) of both sire (father) and dam (mother). It is essential that they are not afflicted with any of the hereditary eye disorders which afflict some specimens of the breed: Hereditary Cataract (HC),

Progressive Retina Atrophy (PRA) and Retinal Dysplasia (RD). These conditions are outlined on pages 27-29 and 56-57.

Responsible breeders take great care and go to great lengths to minimise the risk of these conditions in their stock and, before breeding, ensure that the breeding stock is clear of these complaints. If the breeder cannot furnish you with these certificates, which should have been awarded within the previous six months, then say a polite 'thank you' and seek elsewhere for your puppy. No breeder can guarantee that their stock is absolutely clear of such afflictions, but current eye certificates are a step in the right direction and indicate that at least you are starting out on solid ground with currently sound stock.

Another important factor you should enquire about is the temperament of the breeder's stock. Fortunately American Cockers do not suffer from temperament disorders; aggressive or timid Yankees are rarities, but it is just as wise to ask about this. If the parents of the puppies are there, ask to see them. There is no fun in a cringing, timid dog – no enjoyment in life for either dog or owner. Aggressive dogs are even worse; there is no relaxing with a dog which cannot be trusted. Sound temperament is the essential of a family dog, and this is usually a strong point in the American Cocker's favour. It is, however, policy to seek reassurance from the breeder about his or her stock.

## Healthy signs

It is of great importance that the puppy you buy has been well reared and is healthy. There are various pointers to good health which you should look for when inspecting your prospective puppy. Firstly, well fed, well reared pups are full of life and playfulness. Their coats, which are already developing some thickness by eight weeks of age, should be glossy. Dull, sparse coats are often a sign of worms or ill health. Be wary if you see the litter scratching themselves. Inspect them for fleas and other skin disorders. Thickly coated American puppies often seem to have a little scurf in their coats at this age; this should not be confused with fleas and lice. The eyes should be bright and alert, and there should be no discharge from eyes or nose. Although only babies, the bones should be sturdy and strong; avoid spindly, fragile-boned puppies. Healthy pups should be friendly and outward going by the age of eight weeks. A litter of this age is often quite a 'rough-house' when playing together. This is not aggression, just good health and high spirits. Avoid pups which hide in their box or cringe away from contact. Ensure that the pups have been wormed at least once by this time, and make a note of the dates.

## Papers

If the litter seems to be healthy in all of these respects and you have seen the current eye certificates of the parents, then all is set for you to become the proud owner of an American Cocker. Ensure that you obtain your pup's pedigree and your Kennel Club Registration papers. The responsible and caring breeder will also give you a diet sheet to help you to continue the healthy rearing of your puppy.

**Below:** *From puppy to adult. The appeal of the puppy and the splendour of the fully-coated adult are well illustrated in this study of a proud American Cocker dog and his young son.*

# Chapter Four

# GROOMING YOUR AMERICAN COCKER SPANIEL

N o matter what breed of dog, grooming should become a regular part of its routine. Through regular brushing and combing the dog is kept clean and smart, dead hair is removed, new coat growth stimulated and the skin and muscle tone of the dog improved. The owner, too, will notice the benefits in the decrease of dog hair left on his or her clothing and around the home.

The American Cocker requires regular and thorough trimming and grooming and it would be irresponsible to take on this breed without being prepared to accept this. The American Cocker will need clipping every six to eight weeks, plus frequent grooming between

trims. The owner may choose to take his dog to be professionally clipped at a dog parlour or by a breeder, but this is not the only option. It is quite possible for the pet owner to become proficient enough to trim his or her own dog. Not only is this more economical, but the sense of achievement and satisfaction is much greater. Grooming need not be and should not be a chore to be endured by dog and owner: it should be a

---

**Below:** *Some of the many types of brush available for grooming your dog. Bristle or pin brushes effect the best penetration of the thick coat of the American.*

pleasurable experience for both and certainly the final effect should give the feeling of well-being in the dog and satisfaction to the owner.

## Types of trim

A beautiful American Cocker turned out for the show ring with its long coat gleaming is a superb sight. It takes a lot of time and effort to keep it looking like that, and it is time well spent. However, the pet owner might not find the heavy-coated American quite so practical for everyday family life in town and country. A walk through wet city streets or along woodland paths with a fully coated dog will make one aware of the drawbacks. It need not, however, be an insufferable problem. Many pet owners choose to have their American's coat cut down to a practical length, so that it is easier to maintain and keep clean. I choose to call it a 'utility' trim. With the thinning out of leg and tummy coat the dog can retain its American looks and character but present much less work for the owner.

The show American takes more time and effort; I recommend thorough grooming every other day and much more frequent bathing to cleanse the coat, stimulate new growth and prevent doggy odours. I also feel that the show dog benefits from skilled 'finger and thumb' trimming (or 'handstripping') of the back coat which takes considerably more time than the thinning scissor method recommended for the utility trim. Full instructions on the show trim are given in the chapter on showing in this section. No matter which trim you choose, I hope these basic guidelines will help you along!

## Grooming equipment

The correct equipment will make grooming much easier. Here are some suggestions:

**A firm brush** This is for the back coat. Use this with firm, long strokes working from the neck towards the tail. A hound glove is also suitable for this job.

**A bristle or pin brush** This is used to penetrate the longer leg and tummy hair. A wire brush may be suitable for the heavily coated blacks, but the finer coated buffs and parti-colours require a pure bristle brush.

**A fairly wide-toothed steel comb** This is to penetrate the longer hair and reach the skin, hence preventing matting.

**A fine-toothed comb** This is for combing the back, removing the loose short hair and undercoat and thus helping to maintain a smooth, flat back coat.

## Grooming technique

Grooming should start in the early stages of puppyhood. The American Cocker of eight weeks is already developing its leg and body coat. Be patient and gentle – the first grooming experiences are important in forging the bond between dog and owner and inculcating good (or bad) habits for the future. Your puppy may be brushed and combed, paying special attention to the soft hair behind the ears which can be inclined to matt,

Below: *An adult American in 'pet' or 'utility' trim. The thinned leg and tummy coat make it a very manageable length and easier for the owner to maintain.*

and also the areas under the front legs, another site where knotting frequently occurs.

If you do find knots, do not pull at them roughly; this is painful and frightening for the dog. Work at the knots with your fingers and tease them out gently with the comb, speaking to the dog soothingly. Bad matting can often be eased by the use of one of the preparatory grooming sprays readily available from most suppliers of pet equipment, and at dog shows. Grooming of the armpit area and the tummy can be aided by training the dog to lie on its side. This is also useful for drying the dog after bathing.

Be gentle but firm with the dog who objects to grooming; it must learn that it is not painful and that it must obey its master. A well behaved dog makes grooming so much easier.

### Trimming equipment
If you are going to manage the clipping and trimming of your American, you will also need the following equipment:

**Electric clippers** These are used for clipping the head, ears, front, and area under tail. Clippers with a variety of interchangeable cutting heads of varying degrees of fineness are available. The one-dog pet owner would probably be well advised to buy the much less expensive model with an adjustable clipping head.

**Thinning scissors** These are for thinning out the coat and for blending clipped areas with

non-clipped areas. I recommend the scissors with one plain and one serrated blade.

**Cutting scissors** These are for shaping the feet and general coat shortening.

**Nail clippers** The long coat on an American's legs and feet often prevents the nails from being shortened by the usual method – roadwork. The guillotine type of clipper is safe and does not, generally, cause any distress or discomfort to the dog.

---

### THE UTILITY OR PET TRIM

If you decide that the full coat of your American is too much to manage, then a shorter 'utility' trim is called for. If you are taking your dog to a professional canine beautician for its trim, then ask them to thin down the dog's leg coat and tummy feathering. To have all the furnishings removed is rather drastic and detracts from the 'American' character of the dog; this can be retained with thinned out furnishings.

### Use of clippers
If you have decided that you would like to manage your dog's clipping yourself, I recommend strongly that you should not attempt your first clipping without first having some expert tuition or demonstration.

---

**Below:** *Many types of scissors are available. Trade stalls at major shows are good sites for enquiry and purchase of these.*

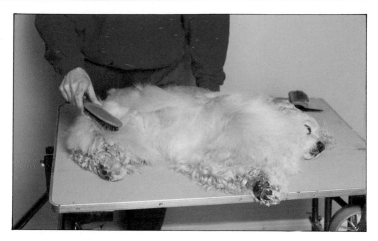

Some canine beauticians do offer lessons in clipping and trimming. If you have bought your puppy from a reputable breeder or exhibitor then it is most likely that help can be received from this source. Watch your teacher carefully; make notes; ask questions; try your hand under supervision.

Go with caution and take your time. Do not press too hard with the clippers. When the time comes for you to attempt your first clipping and you are smitten with fear, you can be consoled by the fact that even the most skilful groomers were once in the same state. Practice makes perfect, and if you make a terrible blunder — take off too much hair or leave the odd bald patch — remember that hair will grow again

**Below:** *Electric clippers with adjustable cutting heads or interchangeable blades. Remember to have them regularly serviced.*

**Above:** *The thick furnishings must be penetrated and all tangles removed – made easier if your dog will lie on its side.*

in time. If using clippers with interchangeable blades, I find that a No10 blade is suitable for the sides of the head, neck and ears. To really clean out the stop on the head, the No15 – a finer, closer blade – is very successful.

### Step-by-step clipping
**Step one** Groom the dog thoroughly before starting the trim, combing out all tangles.

**Step two** Using your electric clippers, clip the sides of the dog's skull then clip the dog's muzzle. Use clippers in the directions shown in **Fig 1**, page 52.

**Step three** Clip the top one-third of the dog's ear leather, both outside

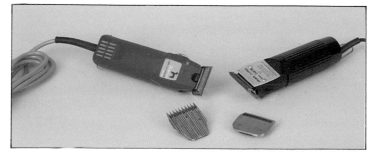

hard brush and
fine comb

danger
areas for
matting

bristle and pin
brush, followed
by wider-toothed
steel comb

1

2

3

and inside. Clip in an upwards direction (**Fig 1**).

**Step four** Locate the dog's chest bone (slightly above and between the forelegs). Clip upwards from this point towards the dog's throat. Clip upwards and outwards to form a V shaped pattern (**Fig 2**).

**Step five** Clip the area beneath the dog's tail.

### The thinning process
Clipping completed, it is now necessary to thin out the dog's thickly coated areas. When using the thinning scissors, always keep the plain edge closest to the dog's skin. Work against the lie of the coat and try to work under the top coat, ie place the scissors, plain side down, **into** the dog's coat as opposed to placing them **on top** of the coat.

As you use the thinning scissors, keep combing out the coat which has been removed by the thinning process. You are aiming for a flat, 'sleek fitting' coat, free from fuzzy and obtrusive ends. You will see the gradual thinning of the coat and the dog's shape gradually re-emerge from under all that hair. The illustration (**Fig 3**) gives guidelines on the areas for thinning and the direction in which you should thin.

Remember:
(1) Scissor **under** the topcoat.
(2) Scissor against the lie of the coat.
(3) Comb out **with** the lie of the coat.

Thin out until you have brought the coat to the length you desire. Leave sufficient tummy coat and trousers to ensure that your dog retains its American type!

### Shaping the feet
After the thinning process, ensure that you have combed out all the loose hair. The loose ends round the feet should now be taken off to give the final touch. Pick up the foot and look at the underside. With your plain scissors remove the hair between the toes, taking great care not to cut the pads.

Next run your hand firmly down the leg, finishing up with your hand completely surrounding the upturned foot. The loose, straggling ends of hair will protrude outside your grip. Trim them off in a circular movement.

Finally, place the foot down and take off any remaining untidy ends.

**Below:** *Use plain scissors to remove the hair between the toes on the underside of the feet.*

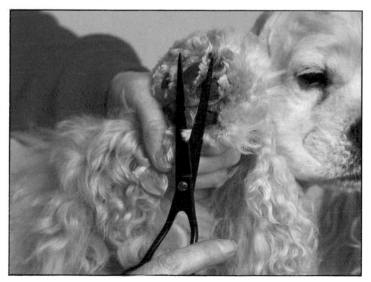

### Shaping the tail

The hair on the American's tail often grows very thickly. Thin the sides and the top of the tail. The underside may be clipped.

### Trimming the nails

Great care must be taken to ensure that the 'quick' is not cut as this causes bleeding, pain and often temporary lameness. The quick can be seen in the nails of buff Americans or parti-colours with white nails, but in black dogs it is not visible. Hold the foot firmly and take off the sharp, pointed ends of the nails.

## BATHING YOUR AMERICAN

### How often?

Of course this will differ with individual circumstances. The 'utility'-trimmed American will need less frequent bathing than its show-coated brother. The longer-coated dog can harbour more dirt, smells and parasites than the short-coated one. Bathing also stimulates coat growth so this is much favoured for show dogs. The pet dog will benefit from a bath every time it is trimmed, say every four to six weeks. Many show dogs receive a weekly bath.

### Preparations

It is absolutely essential that your dog is groomed and tangle-free before it is bathed. A tangled dog will be even more tangled after bathing. Huge knots of damp hair make thorough drying difficult and spoil the lie of the coat. Some people find it useful to place small wads of cotton wool in the ear to prevent water getting into the ear drum. If you do this, ensure that you do not place them too far inside the ear. Remember they must be **removed** after bathing is completed.

### Bathing equipment

**Rubber mat** This is most useful for placing in the sink or bath, providing a better grip for the dog.

**Shampoo** There is a large selection of shampoos available depending on coat type, colour and condition. Many human shampoos are equally

Below: *Drying the dog. Comb gently through the wet coat. The body can then be wrapped in a pinned towel or a nylon tube, as illustrated here, while the leg hair is blown dry. Brush the hair as it is blow dried.*

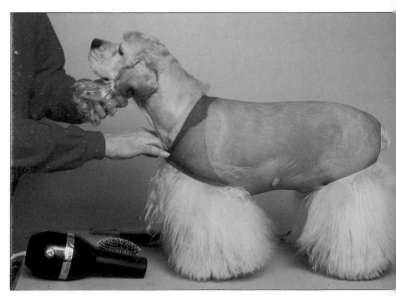

suitable (and often less expensive). If infestation with skin parasites is suspected (see pages 87-88), then a medicated or insecticidal shampoo is required. Follow the instructions carefully with this type of shampoo, particularly regarding dilution, and take great care, as with other types of shampoo, that no shampoo gets into the dog's eyes.

**Conditioner** I find that the application of a creme rinse or conditioner after shampooing not only aids grooming after the bathing but also adds an extra bloom to the coat.

You will find it much easier to apply shampoo and conditioner if it is stored in plastic, nozzle-topped bottles. In this way you can apply the shampoo accurately with one hand whilst maintaining control over the dog with the other.

**Towels** Do not discard your old household towels; they will be very useful for this purpose.

**Dryer** Thorough drying is essential after bathing. The thickness and length of the fully-coated American takes a considerable amount of time to dry and renders the average human hair dryer unsuitable for the job. There are many types of stronger, heavy duty dryers available and it is an essential item for anyone owning more than one American or bathing dogs frequently.

**The bathing process**
Wet the dog thoroughly with luke warm water. Work gradually from the head and ears towards the tail. Massage the shampoo well into the coat, particularly into the thickly coated areas.

After shampooing, rinse the dog thoroughly and apply conditioner if desired, allowing it to remain in the coat for a minute or two before rinsing out.

After the final rinse **squeeze** all the surplus water out of the dog, running your hands firmly down all four legs. Wrap the dog firmly in towels and place it on the grooming table.

**Drying**
Having squeezed all the excess water out of the coat with your hands, now repeat the process with towels. I do not recommend vigorous rubbing with a towel as this often causes tangling of the coat. Squeeze and pat the dog to a damp state, and then comb out its leg and tummy furnishings and ears.

Wrap and pin a towel round the middle of the dog. Some people find that a footless leg cut from a pair of nylon tights a useful alternative. Either of these methods will facilitate the later drying of this area. Now, it is possible to concentrate on drying the other areas. Start with the ears and work methodically drawing one part of the dog at a time and drying it thoroughly.

It is absolutely essential for a good finish to the coat that your comb the area of coat which is being dried. If you have a hand drier you will probably need someone to hold the dog whilst you proceed, especially during the first baths when the dog is not accustomed to the routine. The dog should be trained to stand and lie unassisted, thus helping its owner. A free-standing drier makes drying so much easier as it allows the groomer to have both hands free. A pin brush or wide-toothed comb is best for grooming the damp coat whilst aiding penetration from the drier.

Ensure that the coat is dry to the skin and not just the top coat. A superficially dried coat often 'cotters' or goes wavy, unlike the thoroughly dried coat which retains its straightness and gloss.

After the four legs have been dried, remove the towel or nylon 'tight' from the dog's middle. The back and tummy coat should now be almost dry. Direct the heat flow to this area and brush and comb until dry. Thorough drying of the tummy coat will be helped if the dog lies down on its side.

Once the tummy coat has been dried, turn off the drier, brush out the dog and if there are any loose ends which have appeared, trim them off neatly. You should now have a shining and smart American.

# Chapter Five

# BREEDING: HEREDITARY PROBLEMS

## Why breed?

Many dog owners are often tempted to have a litter from their bitch. Why? I suppose the desire springs from a natural fascination and a love of young puppies. There is often also the desire to retain a puppy from a much loved pet. Many think a litter is necessary for the good of a bitch's health – a view to which I personally do not subscribe. Some commercially-minded individuals believe breeding is an easy way to make money.

I personally believe that far too many dogs of all breeds are produced. There is far too much indiscriminate breeding, resulting in poor quality, untypical specimens. There are many dogs' homes and rescue stations throughout the world full of unwanted dogs, many of them pedigree. Far too often people breed dogs and buy dogs without thinking of the long term responsibilities. Hereditary conditions within a breed are often perpetuated and made worse by ignorant breeders. As for making money from breeding, I think that breeders who see much profit from a well-planned, well-reared litter are few and far between. Stud fees, transport, rearing and advertising costs are apt to swallow up any potential profit.

## The breeder's responsibilities

American Cockers are the most attractive of puppies; it is perfectly understandable that they appeal to the general public. They are pretty, glamorous, status symbols – but, as I have made clear, it takes time and work to keep them in this condition. If you breed from your bitch and sell any puppies from the litter, it is your responsibility to impress upon prospective owners the particular demands of the breed when they are viewing the cuddly bundle of fluff with the appealing eyes.

Much more important is the fact that the American Cocker has its fair share of hereditary problems which must be given the greatest consideration when planning a breeding programme. These problems can only be aggravated by well-intentioned, but often misguided individuals who go blindly ahead without first seeking out vital knowledge about the breed. I have outlined below the serious hereditary problems which must be considered before breeding from your American.

## Hereditary problems

Like many breeds of pure-bred dogs, the American Cocker Spaniel has its share of hereditary problems. In the case of the American Cocker, the most serious afflictions are ocular diseases. There are three major conditions: Hereditary Cataract (HC); Progressive Retinal Atrophy (PRA) and Retinal Dysplasia (RD). It might never be possible to completely eradicate these problems, but responsible breeders work towards reducing them to a lower incidence, to minimise the risk of their occurrence.

American Cocker Clubs throughout the world are concerned with reducing the incidence of these abnormalities, and control schemes to help breeders have been set up. Breeders are encouraged to take their stock to be examined by a veterinarian specializing in ophthalmology. Clearance certificates are given to dogs clear of these hereditary conditions. Breeders are then recommended to send their results to the breed clubs, which publish an Eye Health Compendium, containing the names of clear and afflicted dogs. It is through the sharing of such information that breeders can become aware of the problems and the varying incidence in different bloodlines. The responsible breeder will then try to avoid high-risk bloodliness in his or her breeding plans and thus minimise the risk of occurrence.

**Hereditary Cataract (HC)** This is the most serious and most widespread of the eye afflictions in the breed. See Section One, Chapter Five for full details of the condition.

**Progressive Retinal Atrophy (PRA)** Fortunately, this is not as widespread as Hereditary Cataract; in the UK it is comparatively rare in the American Cocker. Again, see Section One, Chapter Five for further details.

**Retinal Dysplasia (RD)** This, unlike the former two ocular diseases, is a congenital disease (ie present at birth) and therefore can be diagnosed very early in life; puppies can be tested from six weeks of age. Retinal Dysplasia does not usually result in blindness or defective vision in the American Cocker. The disease is caused by folds in the retina (retinal folds).

The fact that the disease does not apparently produce defective vision and that its incidence is relatively low make it a less serious problem than the HC and PRA.

Inheritance is considered to be as a recessive trait. There is considerable disagreement over the use of RD afflicted stock and RD carriers in the breeding programme. It is considered by some breeders and some veterinarians as a trivial complaint; others fear that haphazard use of RD afflicted/carrier stock could result in the disease becoming more widespread.

**Below:** *'When I was your age . . .' An affectionate relationship between father and son, showing a distinct family likeness.*

# Chapter Six

# SHOWING YOUR AMERICAN COCKER SPANIEL

## THE UK BREED STANDARD

**General appearance** Serviceable looking dog with refined chiselled head, strong, well-boned legs, well up at the shoulder, compact sturdy body, wide muscular quarters, well balanced.

**Characteristics** Merry, free, sound, keen to work.

**Temperament** Equable with no suggestion of timidity.

**Head and skull** Well developed and rounded, neither flat nor domed. Eyebrows and stop clearly defined. Median line distinctly marked to

Below: *Hirontower on Broadway exhibiting round skull, short foreface, low ear set and correct eye shape.*

rather more than half-way up crown. Area surrounding eye socket well chiselled. Distance from tip of nose to stop approximately one-half distance from stop up over crown to base of skull. Muzzle broad, deep, square, even jaws. Nose well developed. Nostrils black in black and tans, black or brown in buffs, browns, browns and tans, roans and parti-colours.

**Mouth** Jaws strong with a perfect, regular and complete scissor bite, ie upper teeth closely overlapping lower and set square to the jaws.

**Eyes** Eyeballs round, full and looking directly forward. Shape of eyerims gives a slightly almond appearance. Neither weak nor goggled. Expression intelligent, alert, soft and appealing. Colour of iris dark brown to black in blacks, black and tans,

buffs and creams, and in the darker shades of parti-colours and roans. In reds and browns, dark hazel; in parti-colours and roans of lighter shades, not lighter than hazel; the darker the better.

**Ears** Lobular, set on line no higher than lower part of eyes, feather fine and extending to nostrils, well clothed with long silk, straight or wavy hair.

**Neck** Long, muscular and free from throatiness. Rising strongly and slightly arched.

**Forequarters** Shoulders deep, clean-cut and sloping without protrusion, so set that upper points of withers at an angle permitting wide spring of ribs. Forelegs straight, strongly boned and muscular, set close to body well under scapulae. Elbows well let down, turning neither in nor out. Pasterns short and strong.

**Body** Height at withers approximating length from withers to set on of tail. Chest deep. Lowest point no higher than elbows, front sufficiently wide for adequate heart and lung space, yet not so wide as to interfere with straight forward movement of forelegs. Ribs deep and well sprung throughout. Body short in couplings and flank, with depth at flank somewhat less than at last rib. Back strong, sloping evenly and slightly downwards from withers to set of tail. Hips wide with quarters well rounded and muscular. Body appearing short, compact and firmly knit together,

giving impression of strength. Never appearing long and low.

**Hindquarters** Strongly boned, muscled with good angulation at stifle and powerful, clearly defined thighs. Stifle joint strong without slippage. Hocks strong, well let down; when viewed from behind, hindlegs parallel when in motion or at rest.

**Feet** Compact, not spreading, round and firm, with deep, strong, tough pads and hair between toes; facing truly forward.

**Tail** Customarily docked to three-fifths of tail. Set on and carried on a line with top line of back, or slightly higher, never straight up and never so low as to indicate timidity. When dog in motion merry tail action.

**Gait/movement** Co-ordinated, smooth and effortless, covering ground well.

**Coat** On head, short and fine; on body, medium length, with enough under coating to give protection. Ears, chest, abdomen and legs well feathered, but not so excessive as to hide body lines or impede movement and function as a sporting dog. Texture most important. Coat silky, flat or slightly wavy. Excessive coat, curly, woolly or cotton texture undesirable.

**Below:** *Frank Kane's Sh Ch Doganodogs Dizzy Dame in natural stance. Note the shortness of back and correct coat texture.*

**Colour** Blacks jet black; shadings of brown or liver in sheen of coat undesirable. Black and tan and brown and tan (classified under solid colours) and plainly visible and colour of tan may be from lightest cream to darkest red colour. Amount of tan marking restricted to ten per cent or less of colour of specimen; tan markings in excess of ten per cent undesirable. Tan markings not readily visible in ring or absense of tan markings in any of specified locations undesirable. Tan markings located as follows:

1. A clear spot over each eye
2. On sides of muzzle and on cheeks
3. On underside of ears
4. On all feet and legs
5. Under tail
6. On chest, optional, presence or absence permissible

Tan on muzzle which extends upwards and over and joins highly undesirable. Any solid colour other than black should be of uniform shade. Lighter colouring of feathering permissible. In all above solid colours a small amount of white on chest and throat while not desirable, permissible, but white in any other location highly undesirable.

Parti-colours. Two or more definite colours appearing in clearly defined markings essential. Primary colour which is ninety per cent or more highly undesirable; secondary colour or colours which are limited solely to one location also highly undesirable. Roans are classified as part-colours and may be of any of usual roaning patterns. Tri-colours, any of above colours combine with tan markings. Tan markings preferably located in same pattern as for Black and Tan.

**Size** Ideal height: (The word approximate leaves too much to chance.)
Dogs: 36.25-38.75 cm (14½-15½ in)
Bitches: 33.75-36.25 cm (13½-14½ in)

**Faults** Any departure from the foregoing points should be considered a fault and the seriousness with which the fault should be regarded should be in exact proportion to its degree.

**Below:** *A visualisation of the Breed Standards. The distance from tip of nose to stop should be about one-half the distance from stop to base of skull.*

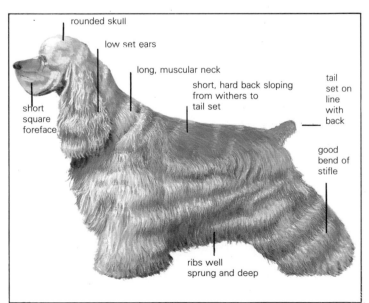

rounded skull

low set ears

long, muscular neck

short, hard back sloping from withers to tail set

tail set on line with back

short square foreface

good bend of stifle

ribs well sprung and deep

**Note**
Male animals should have two apparently normal testicles fully descended into the scrotum.

## EXPLANATION OF THE STANDARD

**General appearance and characteristics** These sections of the standards are quite explicit in stressing some of the most important features of the breed. The terms 'free' and 'merry' underline my earlier remarks about the breed's temperament. The standard calls for a serviceable looking dog, in complete balance or well balanced throughout. These are somewhat vague terms but when pondered over call for the same quality: freedom from exaggeration. As a sporting spaniel the American should be sound enough and sturdy enough to do a day's work in the field. Exaggeration in any one area often brings unsoundness or lack of balance, that almost indefinable element which is so essential in a quality dog. To me, a well balanced dog is one in which every part of the dog is proportionate so that it presents a pleasing and aesthetic picture. A balanced dog looks 'right'. Another vital phrase in this section of the standard is 'well up at the shoulder', highlighting one of the most important physical traits of the breed and a feature which should clearly differentiate it from its English cousin: the topline which in the American should slope from his withers to the set on of the tail. The American is more 'up on front leg' than his English counterpart and this feature is important in contributing to the very distinctive outline of the breed.

**Head and skull** I would stress here the desirability of a good stop between the eyes and a pleasing rise of skull (the dome). These features — allied with the short foreface, the chiselling round the eyes and the eyes themselves — are of the utmost importance for the American breed type. Bony cheeks and an excessively broad, heavy skull detract from the quality of a dog and result in a rather course appearance. The eye of the American Cocker is rather fuller than that of the English Cocker, but an overbold, goggle eye is a most unattractive fault. As for eye colour, apart from the chocolate coloured American where a lighter shade of hazel is permissable, the general principle is, the darker the better.

Although the standard calls for a rounded, well developed skull, it also decries a domed skull, which seems to be something of a contradiction. The skull of the American Cocker is rounded, but again exaggeration into apple headedness is not desirable.

**Ears and neck** The important feature of the ears is the 'set on', ie the point where the ears join the skull. An ear set higher than eye level detracts from the quality of the head and expression of the dog. A good length of neck always adds a touch of quality to a dog's outline but loose skin under the throat is a great detraction.

**Shoulder** Placement of the shoulder is vital in determining a dog's outline, forehand balance and movement. The shoulder blades (scapula) should be clean cut, with their points close at the dog's withers. They should slope forwards at an angle of approximately 45 degrees to meet the upper arm (humerus), forming an angle of approximately 90 degrees as it slopes back to the elbow joint. Insufficient layback of the shoulder, whilst producing an 'up-on-leg' effect, also has the adverse result of producing short necks and narrow fronts. Insufficient layback of the upper arm reduces the dog's length of front stride.

**Body** The dog should be square-bodied, short-backed with well sprung ribs, short coupled and with good depth of body. The American is not all coat and glamour; it should have the substance and strength of a sporting dog. The topline should slope from withers to tailset, and this slope should be maintained when the dog is on the move, a most important trait.

**Hindquarters** The hindquarters must be well angulated, with a good turn of stifle. The well let down hock, indicative of good angulation in the bones of the hindquarters, combines with the well defined withers to produce the much desired slope of topline. The set on of the tail is also important here: 'set on a line with the top line of the back'. This will give a clean, hard line to the back, more severe than the topline of the English Cocker whose tailset is lower, consequently producing a more curving, rounded silhouette.

**Gait/movement** On the move, the American should exhibit a good reach in its front stride, matched by great drive from the rear. The dog should be free going and have some style, a bustling self importance and activity.

**Coat** On coat, it may seem strange to point out that a breed often noted for its coat can have too much of it! Excessive coat is penalised as it

detracts from the sporting function of the breed, impeding movement. It can also detract from the clean lines of the dog. Woolly textured, cotton wool coats, apart from being ugly, are very difficult to keep in order.

**Colour** The section on colour is very detailed, particularly with reference to tan markings on black and tan specimens – the desired proportion of tan and where the markings should be located (this also applies to tri-colours). The poor breeder and exhibitor of black and tans has a very difficult time, trying to find a delicate balance between markings which are not very distinct and those which are excessive. I personally find that heavy tan markings can often make the dog's expression rather hard and mean. In my opinion, type and conformation are much more important as decisive factors in the show ring.

---

## THE US BREED STANDARD

---

**General Appearance** The Cocker Spaniel is the smallest member of the Sporting Group. He has a sturdy, compact body and a cleanly chiseled and refined head, with the overall

dog in complete balance and of ideal size. He stands well up at the shoulder on straight forelegs with a topline sloping slightly toward strong, muscular quarters. He is a dog capable of considerable speed, combined with great endurance. Above all he must be free and merry, sound, well balanced throughout, and in action show a keen inclination to work; equable in temperament with no suggestion of timidity.

**Head** To attain a well-proportioned head, which must be in balance with the rest of the dog, it embodies the following:

**Skull** Rounded but not exaggerated with no tendency toward flatness; the eyebrows are clearly defined with a pronounced stop. The bony structure beneath the eyes is well chiseled with no prominence in the cheeks.

**Muzzle** Broad and deep, with square, even jaws. The upper lip is full and of sufficient depth to cover the lower jaw. To be in correct balance, the distance from the stop to the tip of the nose is one half the distance from the stop up over the crown to the base of the skull.

**Teeth** Strong and sound, not too small, and meet in a scissors bite.

**Nose** Of sufficient size to balance the muzzle and foreface, with well-developed nostrils typical of a sporting dog. It is black in color in the blacks and black and tans. In other colors it may be brown, liver or black, the darker the better. The color of the nose harmonizes with the color of the eye rim.

**Eyes** Eyeballs are round and full and look directly forward. The shape of the eye rims gives a slightly almond-shaped appearance; the eye is not weak or goggled. The color of the iris is dark brown and in general the darker the better. The expression is intelligent, alert, soft and appealing.

**Ears** Lobular, long, of fine leather, well feathered, and placed no higher than a line to the lower part of the eye.

**Neck and Shoulders** The neck is sufficiently long to allow the nose to reach the ground easily, muscular and free from pendulous 'throatiness.' It rises strongly from the shoulders and arches slightly as it tapers to join the head. The shoulders are well laid back forming an angle with the upper arm of approximately 90 degrees which permits the dog to move his forelegs in an easy manner with considerable forward reach. Shoulders are clean-cut and sloping without protrusion and so set that the upper points of the withers are at an angle which permits a wide spring of rib.

**Body** The body is short, compact and firmly knit together, giving an impression of strength. The distance from the highest point of the shoulder blades to the ground is fifteen (15%) per cent or approximately two inches (5 cm) more than the length from this point to the set-on of the tail. Back is strong and sloping evenly and slightly downward from the shoulders to the set-on of the docked tail. Hips are wide and quarters well rounded and muscular. The chest is deep, its lowest point no higher than the elbows, its front sufficiently wide for adequate heart and lung space, yet not so wide as to interfere with the straightforward movement of the forelegs. Ribs are deep and well sprung. The Cocker Spaniel never appears long and low.

**Tail** The docked tail is set on and carried on a line with the topline of the back, or slightly higher; never straight up like a terrier and never so low as to indicate timidity. When the dog is in motion the tail action is merry.

**Legs and Feet** Forelegs are parallel, straight, strongly boned and muscular and set close to the body well under the scapulae. When viewed from the side with the

Left: *This is a parti-colour American Cocker Spaniel. The tan markings are of the desired proportion, according to the Breed Standards, ie readily visible but not excessive, with a clear spot over each eye and on the sides of the cheeks.*

forelegs vertical, the elbow is directly below the highest point of the shoulder blade. The pasterns are short and strong. The hind legs are strongly boned and muscled with good angulation at the stifle and powerful, clearly defined thighs. The stifle joint is strong and there is no slippage of it in motion or when standing. The hocks are strong, well let down, and when viewed from behind, the hind legs are parallel when in motion and at rest. **Feet** Compact, large, round and firm with horny pads; they turn neither in nor out. Dewclaws on hind legs and forelegs may be removed.

**Coat** On the head, short and fine; on the body, medium length, with enough undercoating to give protection. The ears, chest, abdomen and legs are well feathered, but not so excessively as to hide the Cocker Spaniel's true lines and movement or affect his appearance and function as a sporting dog. The texture is most important. The coat is silky, flat or slightly wavy, and of a texture which permits easy care. Excessive or curly or cottony textured coat is to be penalized.

### Color and Markings

**Black Variety** Solid color black, to include black with tan points. The black should be jet; shadings of brown or liver in the sheen of the coat is not desirable. A small amount of white on the chest and/or throat is allowed, white in any other location shall disqualify.

**Any Solid Color Other Than Black** Any solid color other than black and any such color with tan points. The color shall be of a uniform shade, but lighter coloring of the feather is permissible. A small amount of white on the chest and/or throat is allowed, white in any other location shall disqualify.

**Parti-Color Variety** Two or more definite, well-broken colors, one of which must be white, including those with tan points; it is preferable that the tan markings be located in the same pattern as for the tan points in the Black and ASCOB varieties. Roans are classified as parti-colors, and may be of any of the usual roaning patterns. Primary color which is ninety percent (90%) or more shall disqualify.

**Tan Points** The color of the tan may be from the lightest cream to the darkest red color and should be restricted to ten percent (10%) or less of the color of the specimen; tan markings in excess of that amount shall disqualify.

In the case of tan points in the Black or ASCOB variety, the markings shall be located as follows:

1 A clear tan spot over each eye
2 On the sides of the muzzle and on the cheeks
3 On the undersides of the ears
4 On all feet and/or legs
5 Under the tail
6 On the chest (optional, presence or absence not penalized)

Tan markings which are not readily visible or which amount only to traces, shall be penalized. Tan on the muzzle which extends upward, over and joins shall also be penalized. The absence of tan markings in the Black or ASCOB variety in any of the specified locations in an otherwise tan-pointed dog shall disqualify.

**Movement** The Cocker Spaniel, though the smallest of the sporting dogs, possesses a typical sporting dog gait. Prerequisite to good movement is balance between the front and rear assemblies. He drives with his strong, powerful rear quarters and is properly constructed in the shoulders and forelegs so that he can reach forward without constriction in a full stride to counterbalance the driving force from the rear. Above all, his gait is coordinated, smooth and effortless. The dog must cover ground with his action and excessive animation should never be mistaken for proper gait.

**Height** The ideal height at the withers for an adult dog is 15 in (38 cm) and for an adult bitch 14 in (35.5 cm). Height may vary one-half inch above or below this ideal. A dog whose height exceeds 15½ in (39 cm) or a bitch whose height exceeds 14½ in (37 cm) or an adult bitch whose height is less than 13½ in (34 cm) shall be penalized.

**Note:** Height is determined by a line perpendicular to the ground from the top of the shoulder blades, the dog standing naturally with its forelegs and the lower hind legs parallel to the line of measurement.

### Disqualifications
### Color and Markings
**Black Variety** White markings except on chest and throat.
**Any Solid Color Other Than Black Variety** White markings except on chest and throat.
**Parti-Color Variety** Primary color ninety percent (90%) or more.
**Tan Points (1)** Tan markings in excess of ten percent (10%); **(2)** Absence of tan markings in black or ASCOB variety in any of the specified locations in an otherwise tan pointed dog.
**Height** Males over 15½ in (39 cm); females over 14½ in (37 cm).

---

## CHOOSING A SHOW PUPPY

If you go along to a breeder with the aim of buying a prospective show prospect, then apart from looking for general health and well being you must also look for a puppy which measures up closely to the requirements of the breed standard. There are several other factors which you should bear in mind.

There is an old saying which goes: 'You can't get a silk purse from a sow's ear'. It is a sound guideline for breeding show dogs. To produce show stock you first need quality parents. Mediocrities usually breed their own kind. There are exceptions, but the chances of mediocre parents producing a top-notch puppy are extremely remote. Therefore, if you want a show puppy you must go to a breeder who breeds from show quality, winning stock. This does not guarantee show winning progeny, but it increases the chances.

Breeders who breed for the show ring often retain a puppy for themselves. They may also have a waiting list for prospective show stock, therefore you might have to wait for yours. Tell the breeder that you are interested in a show prospect and ask for his or her advice. The reputable breeder will do all he or she can to help you. After all, a satisfied customer with a winning dog of his or her breeding is the best possible advert for the kennel. It gives me the greatest pleasure to see dogs from my kennel winning top awards for their new owners and I am sure other breeders feel the same.

When is it possible to see that a puppy has show potential? There are some breeders who claim to know their winners 'wet', ie as they

---

**Below:** *Show prospects must be trained for the ring. This puppy here practises his show stance.*

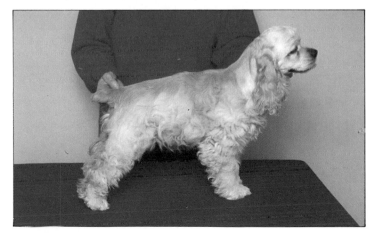

are born. I certainly do not belong to this category. Although it might be possible to see correct conformation and bone structure at this age, I certainly cannot foresee at this time that a puppy will have a good head, dark eyes, good reach of neck, etc. Besides, puppies alter such a great deal as they grow.

## When to choose

At about five weeks of age I start training my pups to stand on a table so they can be examined. By about 8 weeks old the puppy is settled in this routine and can be looked at with a critical eye. I feel that it is at this age that the pup represents a mini-version of the future adult. Before this age it is going through awkward growth stages, and after eight weeks it will go through more gawky growing stages, going leggy and shallow, losing the stop and chiselling in its head and looking generally awful. At about six months old the pup will often start reverting to its former shape. I use the word 'often' advisedly because no matter how promising a puppy is at eight weeks of age, there is **no** guarantee that it will inevitably grow up and achieve its puppy potential. Many are the 'certain champions' of eight weeks who end up as family pets. I choose my show puppies at eight weeks old and then try not to look at them critically until they are about six months old. A gangly puppy of four months might look like a 'no hoper' at that stage of development, but after another few months begins to resume its original promise.

## What to look for

At eight weeks old you can apply the points of the breed standard to your prospective puppy. At this age it should have a good stop between its eyes. Look for a domed skull and low ear set. The foreface should be short and square at this age. Long muzzles should be avoided. Whereas a short foreface may deteriorate and go longer, a long foreface never shortens. The puppy should have a correct and regular 'scissor' bite. Faults in the puppy

bite are usually present in the adult bite.

Look for a good length of neck, sturdy bones and a firm, well-ribbed body. The back should be short and the rib cage should be long. Do not choose a puppy which has a great length of loin, ie the space between the back rib and the set-on of the quarters. Long coupled puppies often become undesirably long backed and develop poor toplines. Most important is the strong, sloping topline and the tail set which should be on a line with the back. A puppy which drops off to its tail set, ie has a rounded rump, will never have the correct topline and tailset which in my opinion is an essential in a show specimen. Look for hindlegs which have well bent stifles with hock joints close to the floor.

It is essential to look at the puppies running around where one can see their general balance and movement. Again, look for a firm, sloping topline, which is retained as the puppy moves. Avoid the puppy with the clamped-down tail; this is a sign of timidity. Many American puppies carry their tails too high at this age. This is not always an indication of a gay tail (too high tail carriage) but often merely a sign of a happy disposition and exuberance. Besides, I feel that a gay tailed dog is preferable to one without the natural exuberant Cocker character.

If you are just setting out as a prospective exhibitor in the show ring, it would be unwise to try to pick out your first show puppy without some expert assistance. Ask a breeder for guidance – and remember this: all of our future hopefuls do not turn out as they promise. Some of our swans turn out to be ducks! No dog is perfect; they all have faults. Your puppy, despite its imperfections, still gives, and demands, loyalty and affection. Remember, a show dog is not an impersonalised abstraction – it must not be discarded or scorned or treated with disaffection merely because it does not measure up to expectations. You must not only be a dog exhibitor; first and foremost you must be a dog lover.

## THE SHOW TRIM

Many of the basic grooming principles already discussed apply to the show dog, but there are several important differences:

1   The show trim implies that the American Cocker is kept with his full luxury of leg and tummy coat, therefore demanding more grooming and more frequent bathing.
2   Whereas a rather fuzzy pet American Cocker can be transformed into a kempt-looking dog with a smart utility trim in a matter of hours, the show trim demands more constant, gradual attention.

**Below:** *The show trim. Muzzle, cheeks, top one third of ear leather (red striped area), front down to breast bone and area beneath tail to be clipped. Blend these clipped areas into the rest of the coat with your thinning scissors – the blue stripes indicate areas which can be thinned. The area within the white line should be handstripped.*

3   Although the basic clipping pattern is the same and some thinning is permissable, the principal difference lies in the art of handstripping the American's back coat, ie plucking the unwanted hair, as opposed to the speedier scissoring techniques. Although some exhibitors do show their dogs heavily scissored, the best, longest lasting effects are achieved with handstripping.

**Handstripping**
The principal area to be handstripped stretches from the crown of the neck, along the back and down the sides of the rib cage.

Many people make the mistake of trying to pull a coat before it is ready. The American's puppy coat is much woollier and fluffier in texture than the desired silky adult coat. The puppy coat usually begins to fall out, or is ready to be pulled out, by eight to nine months of age. To try to do so before this age is pointless, causing discomfort to the dog and achieving poor results, and often hindering the new coat too. Up to this time, combing with a No 6, fine-toothed comb will help to keep the puppy coat in order and remove

some of the thick undercoat.

When the coat is ready to be pulled it is often beneficial to rub some chalk powder into the coat before starting to pluck. This often loosens the coat and helps give some grip to the thumb and forefinger. Take a few hairs between your thumb and forefinger and pull briskly **in the direction of the coat growth**. Proceed from the top of the neck, down to the shoulders and then along the back towards the tail. It is a slow process and it is wise not to attempt the whole job at once. Spend half an hour a day proceeding like this and you will gradually see the disappearance of the puppy wool and the emergence of a flat, shining coat, a sight which gives real satisfaction and reward.

Once you have achieved this state then it is quite easy to maintain. The regular combing with the No 6 comb is often all that is required to maintain the backcoat, or a few minutes each week will be sufficient to pluck out new growth. It is the

first few sessions which demand patience and sadly too many exhibitors seem to lack this. They are in too much of a hurry to get their puppy into the show ring and resort to the thinning scissor method which is convenient, quicker and has pleasing short-term effects. But, in later days, this method often requires more work to maintain it as the back coat, once it has been scissored, often grows more profusely and with a harsher texture than the handstripped coat.

The clipped areas around the tail, under the chin and down the front of the dog can be blended into the handstripped areas with the use of thinning scissors. The trimming of the feet, cleaning of teeth and clipping of nails follows the pattern as suggested for the utility trim.

A word of warning: if you plan to show your dog then all the clipping work should be completed three to four days before the show for the clipped areas to lose their rawness and blend in with the thinned and trimmed areas.

**Below:** *Locating the dog's breast bone, between and slightly above the front legs. Clip upwards from this point, blending in harsh edges with thinning scissors.*

**Right:** *The top knot is trimmed and blended using the thinning scissors. Thin gradually keeping the plain edge of the scissors closest to the dog's skin.*

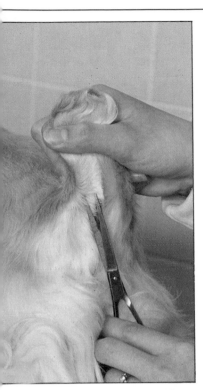

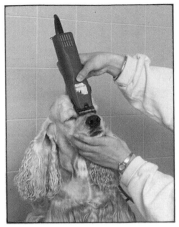

**Above:** *This illustrates the clipping of the head. From the stop – the place between the eyes – clip forwards down the muzzle towards the nose.*

**Left:** *After clipping the area beneath the tail, blend in the hair using the thinning scissors. Then, trim off any loose ends using a pair of plain scissors.*

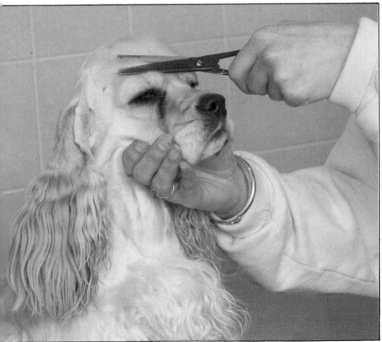

# SO WHAT IS THE DIFFERENCE?

B earing in mind the common ancestry of the two breeds and the relatively recent recognition of their diversity, it is not surprising to see the general similarities.

### Common temperament

Most important is their common characteristics of temperament: the 'merry cocker' is an epithet which can be equally applied to both breeds. They are both squarely built dogs with short backs and good depth of spring of rib. The AKC standard calls for the American Cocker to be shorter than its height at the withers and this does alter the balance somewhat.

### Head shapes

The main differences between the two breeds can be seen in head, topline, tail set and hindquarters. The head shapes of the two breeds

---

**Below:** *The classic head shape of the English Cocker (Mr Happy). The skull is more elongated, less domed and the stop less pronounced than in the American Cocker.*

**Below right:** *In the American Cocker, the rounder skull is about twice the length of its foreface, with the eye slightly rounder and fuller than the English.*

are quite dissimilar. In the English Cocker, the length of foreface is balanced by the length of skull from stop to occiput. The skull is more elongated and less domed than that of the American. The stop is less pronounced. The American's rounder skull is approximately twice the length of its foreface; thus there is a completely different balance to the head. The American's eye is also somewhat rounder and slightly fuller than that of the English Cocker.

**Topline, tail set, sweep of stifle**
The topline and tail set provide the most significant differences. The American Cocker should be 'well up at the shoulder'. This frontal elevation of the American is one of its distinguishing traits. It has more

height on the front leg than its English cousin and thus it should slope gradually down from the point of the withers to the root of the tail. The tail should be set on level with the back; there should be no slope downwards over the rump to the set on. This clean, hard topline is accentuated by the sweep of the American Cocker's stifle and second thigh, which is greater than the English Cocker's. Thus the whole outline and stance of the American Cocker is altered. It is these features of high withers, sloping topline, higher set tail and sweep of stifle which enable you to differentiate.

The English Cocker Spaniel should have a level topline, both standing and on the move. Its tail is

**Above:** *The English Cocker is more cobby and solid than the American with a less pronounced sweep of stifle and broader second thigh. It should have a level topline, with the tail set on slightly lower than the line of the back.*

**Above right:** *The American is distinguished by its high withers, a sloping topline, the tail set on level with the back, ie no roundedness of rump, and a greater sweep of stifle and second thigh than the English Cocker.*

set on slightly lower than the line of the back so there is a pleasantly rounded rump, an anathema in the American Cocker, but one of the essences of English Cocker type. The stifles of the Cocker should be well angulated with hocks low set, but there is a less pronounced sweep of stifle and a broader second thigh than is found in the American Cocker. The elevated front and sweeping lines of the American Cocker lend it an elegance which would be foreign to English Cocker type. The English Cocker is more solid, more cobby, less streamlined than its American counterpart.

**Height and weight**
In the pioneering days of the breeds in America, it was the difference in weight between the two types which was the biggest bone of contention, the American type being much lighter and smaller than the authentic English type. Nowadays, the size disparity has almost gone; the Standards call for a mere ½in (6mm) difference between the two breeds, the English Cocker being slightly the taller.

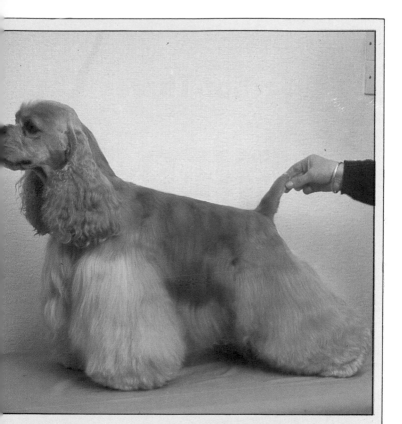

## Coat pattern

Perhaps the most noticeable difference is the coat pattern. Although the coat texture of both breeds is identical, flat and silky, yet the profusion of tummy coat and leg furnishings on the American mark it out immediately. However, even with the coat cut down, the body qualities and lines of the American are still quite distinctive.

## Movement

On the move, the differences are still apparent. The American should maintain its sloping topline, with its tail level with or just above the level of the back. Its greater angulation gives it tremendous rear drive and reach. The English Cocker, also a free moving dog, does not have the same extravagance of gait. Its topline should remain level and its tail carriage should not come above the level of the back.

## Not so different?

To the uneducated eye, the differences might appear slight, but to the Cocker enthusiast, these details are paramount in stamping breed type. It is an unfortunate fact that in the United Kingdom many of the early judges approved to judge the American Cocker Spaniel were people very experienced in judging the English Cocker Spaniel. Hence, it took that much longer for correct American Cocker type to be recognised, appreciated and established in the United Kingdom. Fortunately, for American Cocker enthusiasts, that situation now seems to be improving.

Each breed has its own fervent admirers and devotees, but putting the slight differences of physiology aside, as exemplified here, both parties would agree that the Cocker Spaniel, English and American, is a great little dog!

# Section Three

# GENERAL CARE OF COCKER SPANIELS

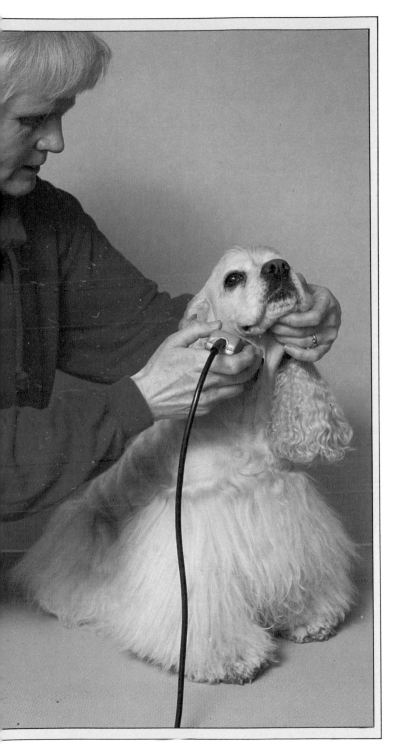

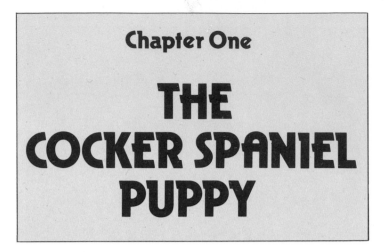

# Chapter One

# THE COCKER SPANIEL PUPPY

## CARE OF THE PUPPY

### Sleep

Make the decision as to where you want your dog to sleep before you bring it home. Most owners plan to let the puppy sleep in the kitchen, or 'utility' room, and these are really the most suitable places. A strong cardboard box large enough for the puppy to be able to lie down, with the front cut down, makes an ideal bed at this stage, progressing to a permanent bed or basket once the puppy has passed the teething phase. Make the box warm and comfortable with a woolly blanket or soft cushion.

Place the box inside a fine wire-mesh pen, or a home-made cardboard pen made from strong boxes, covering the floor area with newspaper where the puppy can relieve itself on waking.

The first night can be the most difficult time for both the owner and the puppy, as it will most certainly feel lonely, missing the company of its mother and litter-mates. Opinions vary on the advisability of having the puppy in the bedroom. Many owners do, and it must be a matter of individual choice. But once started it is difficult to reverse. So unless you are sure you want your

Below: *This new arrival in the family has a cardboard box for its bed, with a woollen blanket, placed in a warm, safe corner.*

dog with you for the rest of its natural days, then do not start it!

In the same way that the human baby needs a lot of rest, so does the small puppy. By the time it arrives in its new home, it will probably need to sleep for quite long periods between meals. It is as necessary to allow the puppy to do so as it is its human counterpart. It is always better, if possible, to allow the puppy to waken naturally from a sleep rather than to wake it up, even if it is a mealtime. The puppy will be refreshed and you will know that it has had enough sleep for a while.

Every week will see a reduction in the amount of sleep required, and by the time the puppy has reached five to six months of age, a short nap at regular intervals will be all it needs during the daytime.

## Feeding

Follow your breeder's diet sheet for at least the first few days to avoid upsetting the puppy's digestive system. Always feed at the same times every day in a quiet, calm environment. The food should not be too hot nor too cold.

Below are some suggested diets for puppies, progressing from two months to one year. Fresh water must be available at all times.

## Handling

How you handle an eight week-old puppy is very important; rough or careless handling at this age can scar it mentally for a long time – maybe for life in extreme cases.

Always pick the puppy up with your left hand under its hindquarters and the right hand controlling the front legs. Never pick it up by the front legs only or by the scruff of its neck. The latter, if done frequently, can cause the puppy to become loose-skinned under its chin – a definite disadvantage should you ever wish to show your dog.

Always be careful that the puppy does not fall to the ground – children should only be allowed to play with the puppy on the ground.

---

**——— Suggested puppy diets from 2 months to one year ———**

*2-4 months*
**Breakfast:** Wholewheat cereal soaked in half milk, half water, with the addition of egg yolk and a teaspoon of honey or brown sugar.
**Lunch:** 3-4ozs (85-113g) raw minced meat with a small amount of soaked puppy meal.
**Tea:** Similar to breakfast omitting egg yolk.
**Supper:** As lunch; or tinned puppy food; or fish; or chicken – plus a little ground dry mixer.
In addition, give daily a multi vitamin/mineral supplement.

*4-6 months: The number of meals can be reduced now to three per day, as follows.*
**Breakfast:** Dry mixer – a good handful at 4 months and increase until two handfuls are given at 6 months. Plus a drink of half milk, half water and egg yolk as before.
**Late Lunch:** 4-6oz (113-170g) meat – chicken or tinned dog food – with a good handful of mixer or meal soaked or dry.
**Early Supper:** As lunch.
Continue with the vitamin/mineral supplement as directed on pack.

*6 months-1 year: Most dogs now require two meals a day but if your pet appears to miss the early morning feed, by all means carry on until it is rejected, or gradually wean the dog off it.*
**Lunch:** 8ozs (227g) meat – fish, chicken or tinned food – with one and a half handfuls of meal or mixer.
**Supper:** As lunch. Supplements as before.

## Inoculations

At approximately 12 weeks of age all puppies must be inoculated against Hepatitis, Leptospirosis, Distemper and Canine Parvovirus. Up until this time, the antibodies provided by their own dam have given them protection and would, in themselves, inhibit the vaccine from taking effect. These vaccinations are given in two injections administered two weeks apart. Not until your puppy has received its second dose is it safe to take it for walks in the street or to meet other dogs.

There is also a vaccine against rabies, recommended for dogs living in countries where the disease exists. Rabies vaccinations are required by law for dogs in the United States. In the United Kingdom and Australia, which are free of rabies, this particular vaccination is obviously unnecessary.

## Socialization

It is very important, at as young an age as is practical, to accustom young puppies to everyday events – unfamiliar noises, people and animals can be very frightening when encountered for the first time.

Most breeders will have exposed their puppies to everyday sights and sounds, such as household equipment and visitors to the house – including children. In the few weeks between the arrival of the puppy in your household and the completion of its vaccination programme (see above), it is not desirable to expose it to health risks by allowing it to exercise on ground used by other dogs. It is therefore difficult to socialize the very young puppy without risking its health. I advise the buyers of my own puppies during this period to take them out in their cars, to stop in busy places and to carry the puppy about in shopping centres. In this way it will absorb the sights and sounds without being in direct contact with the main sources of infection, ie the ground and rubbing noses with other dogs.

As soon as the puppy is fully vaccinated, you can then begin to introduce your puppy to many more situations. A walk in the park is another great adventure, and it is here that you and the puppy will start to make friends with other dogs. But do be careful to protect the puppy from any aggressive big dogs – a bad experience at this age can have a lasting effect.

A good plan is to enrol yourselves at a local dog training class. Some are primarily set up for people wanting to show their dogs, and the exercises are aimed to teach both dog and owner what is required in the show ring. However, they are excellent places to let your puppy meet other dogs and people, and most classes or clubs are quite willing for pet owners to take part even though they do not intend to show their dog – the only pitfall being that you may be bitten by the 'show bug'.

Other training clubs or classes specialize in teaching basic obedience, in some cases progressing to competitive obedience and agility. The classes will again serve as a good socialization basis as well as teaching your dog to understand and respond to basic commands. They will also help you to get to know the temperament of your dog and decide which activity the animal is best suited to, in order to fulfil its potential.

## TRAINING

### House training/breaking

This must begin as soon as you take the new puppy home. The sooner you establish a pattern in the puppy's mind as to the correct place to go for its toilet, the better and less confusing it will be for the puppy.

If possible, arrange to collect your new puppy during the morning. Have its food ready before you go to collect the puppy, and when you arrive home, take it into your garden or suitable piece of open ground. After a few minutes to explore its new surroundings and, hopefully, relieve itself, feed the puppy its midday meal. Do not take the puppy

**Right:** *This well trained young adult has been taught to sit at its owner's side when out at exercise in a public place. It is essential for the owner to have control when the dog is off the lead, for its own safety.*

**Centre:** *The next stage is to teach the dog to sit and stay when the owner is at a distance. This can be achieved by gradually backing away with your hand raised, using the 'stay' command in a firm tone of voice.*

**Below:** *Following on from the 'sit' and 'sit stay', the next step is to train your dog to come when called in all circumstances. The promise of a titbit and lavish praise will encourage the dog to obey your commands.*

into the house until it has passed a motion and relieved itself. When it does, praise the dog lavishly.

Of course, at night a different pattern of behaviour will be necessary in the early weeks, and until the puppy is old enough to go through the night without needing to relieve itself. The puppy can use the newspaper surrounding its bed – most puppies will not soil their own bed – until, as time goes on, it will gradually learn to wait until morning.

During the daytime, the more vigilant you are in watching the signs, such as circling and sniffing around when you can swiftly take the puppy outside, the sooner it will get the message. Remember to praise the puppy when it goes outside. If it makes a mistake indoors and you catch it in the act, a sharp 'no' and an immediate journey out to the garden will hopefully teach the puppy that the house is not the place to relieve itself. If you do not see the puppy actually 'in the act', then it is useless to scold it afterwards; it will not associate the 'bad deed' with your cross tone of voice. It is important to emphasise that dogs only understand **tone** of voice, not the words; use tone to differentiate between scolding and praising.

The puppy is bound to have lapses, even when you think it has learned, and however annoying it is this is one of the inevitabilities of having a young puppy.

Ideally, every dog should have its own garden, however small. But many dogs do live happy, healthy lives in flats, with responsible owners providing sufficient opportunity for exercise outside. In young puppyhood, being a flat-dweller does cause extra housetraining/breaking problems. Train the puppy to use newspaper,

or a special tray with absorbent 'litter' (as used for cats) until its vaccination programme is completed and you can take it for walks outside, at least four times a day to avoid accidents.

**Lead training**
Lead training for the pet puppy can start early if you have a garden, even though it is not possible to extend it to roads, public parks or other places where dogs are exercised, until after the vaccination programme is completed. Give the puppy short periods on the lead daily – only five minutes per session. At first, it will either be a tug-of-war or the puppy will sit down and refuse to move. Be patient and encourage the dog with a titbit. It will soon come to walk at your side. By the time you go for proper walks, the puppy should be fully confident in a short time. An extending lead is also useful in the early days in public places, until the puppy is used to coming when called.

Right: *A young Cocker being taught to walk to heel on a loose lead. This is essential for the pet and show Cocker. Training classes will help to teach both the puppy and the owner how to give and respond to basic commands.*

## HOME HEALTH CARE

The Cocker Spaniel puppy requires regular attention to be paid to the following areas.

### Eyes
Use a piece of moist cotton wool to wipe any discharge from the eyes, mainly found in the morning. If the eyes look sore or ulcerated, it may be necessary to use an ointment for a short time. Consult your veterinarian.

### Ears
A lot of harm can be done by poking about inside the ear with such things as cotton wool buds, in the belief that you are cleaning the inside of the ear. More than likely, you will introduce a foreign body or organism where none previously existed. All that is needed is to clean the visible part of the ear **when needed** – with moist cotton wool. If there is any discharge or smell, consult your veterinarian.

### Mouth
The teeth in young Cockers do not normally require any special care. If, however, there is a build up of tartar, then it is advisable to let your veterinarian remove this. It can cause problems with the gums if left unattended for too long. You can undertake regular cleaning of your dog's teeth using a canine toothpaste, but is only practical if your pet is receptive to your efforts.

Another problem which occasionally occurs is in the crevice on the lower jaw. In some Cockers this seems to be deeper than in others, and it is in the first mentioned that it is possible for food particles to become lodged. If this happens it makes the crevice both

Below: *Tartar can be removed from the young Cocker's teeth using a dental scaler, providing your dog has enough patience.*

sore and foul smelling. Regular wiping out with a mild disinfectant or antiseptic cream will help to prevent it. If, however, it has become well established before you notice it, then it may require veterinary treatment.

### Feet

The cocker's feet do not normally pose many problems. It is a good idea to keep the nails fairly short, and this is best done by a veterinarian, when necessary, since it is important not to cut the 'quick' in the nail, visible only in white nails, to avoid bleeding and pain. It is important to keep the feet trimmed in order to minimise the amount of grit and dirt brought into the house. This includes the hair which grows on the underside of the foot, between the pads. Unless it is kept short, it can become matted and form hard lumps. This is very uncomfortable for the dog, and

rather tricky to remove unless you have a very patient dog.

---

### PARASITES

---

The young Cocker Spaniel is susceptible to the following parasites, and you will need to regularly check your dog for signs of infestation. See also Chapter Two on parasites of the adult Cocker.

### Roundworms

Most puppies have these worms (**toxocara canis**); they are born with the larvae in their bodies, which develop into adult worms by the time the puppy is two weeks of age. The adult worm can be up to 5in (13cm) long and produces microscopic eggs which can exist in the ground or in your home for a very long time. They are a health hazard, particularly to young children in warm, damp conditions.

As mentioned before, you should

---

**Below:** *The use of plier-type nail clippers to shorten the nails. The quick is visible in white nails but black nails are best left to the veterinarian.*

**Below right:** *It is important to regularly trim the hair on the underside of the foot with care, to prevent matting and the formation of hard lumps.*

make a note of the dates when the puppy was wormed when you collect it from the breeder. Ideally, it will have been wormed at two and a half to three weeks of age, and subsequently at two-week intervals. The worming treatment should continue every two weeks until the puppy reaches three months of age, then again at six months of age. Visit your veterinarian to discuss the worming programme and to obtain the necessary treatment – usually in tablet form.

## Ear mites
These parasites live on skin debris on the surface of the ear canal. They can cause intense irritation and the production of reddish brown crusts. The infection is highly contagious and is especially prevalent in young animals. Mineral oils combined with an insecticide are effective as long as the treatment is maintained for a four-week period. The dog's environment should be treated as thoroughly as the dog itself.

## Cheyletiella mites (walking dandruff)
This is a parasite that can cause unpleasant irritation to the owner as well as the pet host. The mites live only on the host and consequently are easier to deal with. The mites and eggs can be seen with a magnifying lens, but the appearance of fine dandruff on the coat gives a clue to their presence. Most insecticides are effective but should be applied three times at weekly intervals.

## Scabies (sarcoptic mange)
This mite produces an intensely itchy, non-seasonal, transmissible infection. The mites burrow in the superficial layers of the skin, and can live on human beings for at least six days. The infection is highly contagious and young animals are particularly susceptible.

As the mite lives most of its life below the surface of the skin, it can be difficult to diagnose, even by repeated skin scrapings examined microscopically. Your veterinarian may make a diagnosis purely on the appearance of the patient. Although insecticides are effective, hair will need to be clipped away and other medications used to relieve irritation and remove skin scale. Again, the dog's environment should be treated with an insecticide.

# Chapter Two

# THE ADULT COCKER SPANIEL

## CARE OF THE ADULT

### Feeding
When the Cocker Spaniel reaches one year of age, most owners find it more convenient to feed a main meal once a day from now on, with dry biscuits only as a supplementary meal.

### Main meal
At least 10-12 ozs (283.5-340g) of meat or fish with two handfuls of mixer or meal. Feeding time must obviously fit in with your own commitments, but generally early evening is considered the best time.

### Quantities
Dogs, like people, are individuals, and what will make one fat will leave another rather too thin. Food requirements also vary according to the amount of exercise that the dog gets – a country Cocker or gundog will need a good deal more 'fuel' than the pet city-dweller. So, it is not possible to be explicit regarding amounts – trial and error are the only way to arrive at the ideal regime.

Cockers in the main are a greedy breed, so do not be blackmailed into giving too much by an over anxious dog. It very unkind to make your dog too fat – in later life it could suffer from heart problems, as well as the extra strain on its joints in old age.

Fresh water should be available at all times.

### Exercise
The amount of exercise needed by an adult Cocker is very flexible. Try to be fairly consistent. For example if you intend to go for a long walk every day – regardless of the weather – then your Cocker will be very happy to go with you. If, however, you are unable to spare more than a half an hour each day, then that will be enough for most Cockers. If the dog seems to need more exercise than you can give it, then it is surprising how far a dog will run in its own garden chasing a ball.

If you live in a flat, it is absolutely essential to set aside time each day to exercise your pet in the local park or a suitable open space. A few words of warning, however. It is very dangerous for children to be in sole charge of any dog, however well-behaved or well trained. The dog has only to be frightened by an unusual sound or the sight of a cat for it to pull at its lead and run away from the child who probably has not the ability or strength to hold onto it. The many possible consequences range from a dead or injured dog to a tragic accident involving human injury.

**Right:** *Cockers love to chase a ball – some are more patient than others! A lot of exercise can be given in this way in a small garden. Take care to use a ball large enough not to be swallowed.*

## HOME HEALTH CARE

### Eyes

If the eyes are inflamed or discharging pus, look for foreign bodies such as grass seeds, then bathe with cotton wool and cool water.

### Ears

These should always be pink and clean, without any unpleasant odour. Use moist cotton wool dipped in almond or olive oil to clean inside the ear, but on no account probe deep into the ear recess. If this recess looks dirty and has an unpleasant odour, a visit to a veterinarian is necessary.

### Anal glands

These are located each side of the anus and should be regularly checked as, unless kept clear, they can become blocked often causing an abscess to form. If you see any signs of your Spaniel pulling itself along the ground while sitting down, or running around after its tail, it is wise to examine these glands. Mild cases are quite easy, if somewhat unpleasant, to deal with. As these glands are situated close to the anal passage, with pressure from your thumb and finger exerted each side

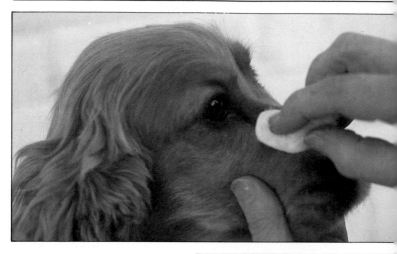

**Above:** *The eyes should be examined each morning. Use a moist cotton wool pad to remove any discharge or excess fluid accumulated during sleep. Also examine the eyes for injury or soreness.*

**Centre:** *The outer part of the ear should be regularly examined and any discharge should be removed with cotton wool. Do not probe beyond the visible part.*

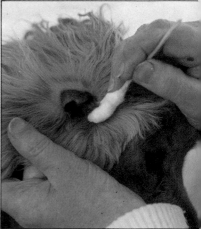

**Below:** *Teeth regularly brushed with canine toothpaste should not accumulate tartar. Your dog should be receptive to this treatment if accustomed to it from its early days in life.*

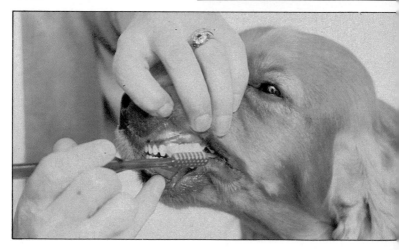

of the anus, they will quickly empty. It is a good idea to ask your veterinarian or the breeder to show you this method, which will enable you to prevent any further trouble in the future.

## Teeth

Always make sure your Spaniel's teeth are in good condition by regular brushing at least once a week using a canine toothpaste.

A careful watch should be kept on the state of the teeth. Any sign of decay or redness of the gums will need expert attention.

Retention of baby teeth can cause long-term problems with the permanent teeth. As a general guide, when all the permanent teeth have erupted – from six to seven months of age – the baby teeth should all have fallen out. If there are any baby teeth left at this stage, contact your veterinarian who will arrange for them to be removed under general anesthetic. A full complement of permanent teeth amounts to 42. In the upper jaw, there should be six incisors, and two canines, one on each side of the incisors. Behind each canine are four premolars on each side, making 20 in all. In the lower jaw, the distribution is identical except for the molars, of which there are three on each side making 22 teeth in all.

## Nails

Cut the nails using strong nail clippers or a special guillotine cutter for dogs' nails. If the nail is light in colour, it is usually possible to see and remove the dead section, taking care not to cut into the bloodline. Black nails are much more difficult, so cut a little at a time. If you do cause the nail to bleed, a dab of permanganate of potash or a styptic pencil will stop the bleeding quite quickly. After cutting the nails, file them smooth with a canine nail file.

## PARASITES

The adult Cocker Spaniel has a range of internal and external parasites, in addition to those detailed in Chapter One.

## Tapeworms

Seek veterinary advice when you suspect tapeworms. They are not directly a health hazard to the family (with one rare exception – see below), but proprietary remedies are rarely effective. The worm needs a secondary host, usually a rodent or flea, to complete its lifecycle. A sign of infection is the appearance of segments of the worm crawling around the dog's anus; they resemble grains of rice.

In areas where hydatid disease is present, regular tapeworm doses should be administered. This tapeworm of dogs is contracted from sheep or deer, and the eggs can infect people.

There are few signs of illness associated with tapeworms in dogs, except in heavy infestation when diarrhoea and weight loss occur.

## Heartworms

These are parasitic worms that are found in dogs' hearts. Dogs are the only mammals commonly affected, and the worm is transmitted by a mosquito. It is found in Africa, Asia and in large areas of the US, particularly the East Coast. In areas where the disease is endemic, daily preventative treatment is essential during the mosquito season. Seek local veterinary advice, and have yearly blood tests to confirm freedom from the infection.

## Fleas

These are very common, and they are not particular about where they live or who they bite. They have increased with the advent of central heating and fitted carpets. Fleas do not need to live on you or your pet; they just need a warm-blooded body to feed off when they are hungry. Because they are small and active, you may not actually see them. But you can spot where they have been by noticing the dark brown droppings when you are grooming.

Flea control is an important part of pet care. They can cause skin problems if your pet is allergic to their bite, and they can also cause you to have irritating red spots. Insecticides are now available which actually inhibit flea reproduction – a great advance. It is vital to treat your dog and its environment at the same time. When using insecticides, follow the manufacturer's instructions carefully. These products must kill the fleas but not the host.

### Demodectic mange
This is a curious parasite which can exist in large numbers of dogs without causing symptoms. When it does, treatment can be lengthy and difficult. Most animals can now be cured, although because the illness may represent an immune failure, dogs having had the disease should not be bred from, unless the condition was only transient. Seek expert veterinary advice.

### Lice (prediculosis)
Lice are spread by direct contact or by contaminated brushes and combs. They accumulate under mats of hair around the ears, neck and body openings causing intense irritation. Since the insects are only $^1/_{10}$ in (3mm) long, they are difficult to see. If you suspect infestation, bathe your dog using an insecticidal shampoo at weekly intervals and clip matted hair away. Lice live and breed entirely on the dog, so it is not vital to treat the dog's environment as well.

### Ticks
Dogs can pick up ticks by running through grass, woods or sandy beaches. These blood-sucking insects bury their barbed mouths firmly into the dog's skin, causing irritation and often resulting in secondary skin infections. To remove adult ticks, soak them with ether, surgical spirit or tick spray. This will loosen the head and mouthparts to enable the removal of the whole insect with tweezers. The dog can be regularly bathed in a tick dip to prevent infestation, especially if it is in contact with sheep. The dog's environment should be vigorously disinfected as in some countries ticks transmit serious diseases such as anaplasmosis and babesiosis, and can cause tick paralysis.

---

**Below:** *This twelve year old may have a few white hairs, but is fit and healthy – and has recently sired a litter of puppies!*

# THE COCKER IN OLD AGE

Dogs, unlike humans, do not know when they are old; they only know how they feel. It is the owner who is aware when their formerly active dog begins to slow down. It is at this stage, when they need extra care. The amount of exercise should be adjusted so that it does not become over tired, especially if it shows any sign of arthritis and begins to limp during or after exercise.

It is necessary to make sure the dog is dried well and does not sit about in a wet coat.

## Diet
The dog's diet may need adjusting so there is less strain on its digestive organs. If it has been fed one meal a day, it is a good idea to split it into two smaller meals, but do it gradually. If you have been feeding raw meat, then a light cooking will make it easier for the dog to digest. It is absolutely necessary to avoid overweight in the elderly dog, for any strain on its heart will shorten its lifespan.

## Health problems
Excessive drinking is usually a sign that the kidneys are not working as well as they were. In the case of a bitch which has not been spayed, this could be a sign of impending pyometra (inflammation of the womb). This condition requires prompt treatment from your veterinarian, either in the form of antibiotics or an operation to remove the reproductive organs.

Another condition some elderly dogs develop is diabetes. This is treatable in many cases, but does involve an injection of insulin daily. Your veterinarian will show you how to do this, if you are prepared to undertake it.

The dog's hearing is often affected in old age. The formerly obedient dog will gradually ignore you when you call it; always give it the benefit of the doubt. The dog may also bark more than usual.

Likewise, eyesight is apt to deteriorate due to the formation of cataracts (a normal ageing process in all animals), so make allowances.

If your formerly sensible pet's behaviour develops uncharacteristic patterns, this may mean that the blood supply to its brain may not be quite as good as it was.

Veterinary science has developed greatly in the use of drugs to help all conditions. Always take the advice of your veterinarian.

## The final goodbye
I write this text with a very heavy heart. Only today I had to have a beloved elderly bitch put to sleep. The decision to face this difficult action never gets any easier. After many years of keeping dogs, I know that awful sinking feeling when the time draws near. You have to face the fact that you now have to part with a friend and companion of many years.

The one kindness we can give our pets that we cannot do for their human counterparts is to avoid unnecessary suffering when a health problem becomes beyond veterinary help. Your veterinarian will know when the time has come, and will perform the task with skill and sympathy. There is no distress to the dog if its owner holds the dog – and this is the very least we can do for it. But if you are able, take a relative or friend with you. Or better still, have your veterinarian come to you. A large dose of anesthetic is administered painlessly.

The decision to replace an only dog is not easy, and a very individual one. Some people find it very hard to live without a pet and seek a new friend very soon, whilst others find it impossible to replace an old and loved friend for several weeks or months. The choice is yours alone, but whatever you decide, do not feel disloyalty to the dog which has gone. The greatest compliment you can pay your old pet is to seek to find another to take its place.

Perhaps a different colour will help to avoid comparisons, but do not be afraid to have one of the same colour – dogs are such individuals that character is of greatest importance.

# Chapter Three

# VETERINARY CARE

This chapter is written in the hope that the pet owner will be able to distinguish between ailments that can be dealt with at home and those that should not be attempted by anyone other than a veterinarian.

## EMERGENCIES

In these days of highly effective vaccines to prevent the major illnesses of dogs such as Distemper, Hard Pad, Hepatitis, Leptospirosis and the highly infectious and dangerous Parvovirus, it is unusual for a properly vaccinated and boosted animal to be affected by any of them. Alas, there are a few dogs who do not develop a full immunity for some reason or other. It is wise to be aware of the symptoms just in case your dog is one of the unfortunate group which is not fully immune.

The owner who knows his or her dog's normal behaviour will soon become aware of any deviation, such as sickness, diarrhoea, listlessness, loss of appetite, coughing and sneezing. Any of these symptoms can be serious, and are best referred to a veterinarian, particularly in a dog under one year. Time can be of the essence; delay can be dangerous. Most veterinarians will not mind if you telephone for advice, and he will arrange to see your dog if he thinks it necessary.

### Accidents
Any accident involving an animal is to say the least upsetting – the more so if you are the owner. Try not to panic; the calmer you can appear to the dog, the more reassured it will be. In the case of a road accident, when a dog has been hit by a car or motor-cycle, the less it is moved the better, until help in the form of the Police or a veterinarian arrives. By all means deal with a bleeding wound, using a pad of cotton wool soaked in cold water and applied with pressure by means of towel or bandage to the bleeding point, as if left unattended, the dog may bleed to death. If there is no obvious sign of bleeding or broken limbs, then it may be quicker to take the dog straight to a veterinary surgery where it can be treated as soon as possible.

### Fighting wounds
If, at any time, your dog gets involved in a fight or is attacked whilst out at exercise by a bigger dog, the first thing to do is to find the owner of the aggressor so that between you, you can separate them. A pair of leather gloves will protect your hands, it being very easy to be bitten by one or other of the dogs. Once parted, they are best kept apart, so always put both dogs on leads to prevent further confrontations. Bites are invariably infected, so the dog will require antibiotic treatment.

## Poisoning

If you suspect that your dog has eaten any kind of poison, then this should be dealt with at once by a veterinarian. If possible, tell him or her what you think the dog has eaten. Slug bait (Metaldehyde) and rat poison (Warfarin) are common poisons.

A safe, first-aid measure is a small piece of washing soda (about the size of a nutmeg) administered immediately, which will cause rapid vomiting and thereby the removal of toxic substances. This is a good and safe procedure for pet owners.

## Burns and scalds

It is dependent on the severity of the burn as to whether or not you need to call your veterinarian immediately. Personally, I would rather be safe than sorry – it is very difficult to determine to what extent the burn has done its damage. But if the burn is obvious, first-aid treatment should be given immediately in the form of cold water. Apply with a towel or flannel, or in the case of a severely scalded dog, immerse in a bath of water until help arrives.

**Below:** *Regular health checks are advisable and can be combined with your annual visit to the vet for vaccination boosters.*

## Stings and bites

Wasps, bees and mosquitoes are all capable of stinging dogs. Indeed, many dogs seem fascinated by these insects and snap at them. This can lead to a bite or sting in, or on, the mouth. Remove the sting with a pair of tweezers if it is visible. Apply a saline solution or mild antiseptic. If the swelling is large and inside the mouth, it is safer to let the veterinarian see the dog. He can give an antihistamine injection to reduce the swelling, which could cause breathing problems. The most dangerous bite is that of the adder – found in some areas more than others – producing a large swelling on the paw, or throat region. These bites are seldom fatal. Adders are shy creatures, and will normally retreat at the approach of any animal or human. However, they are fond of basking in the sunshine, and should they be trodden on accidentally, will, without doubt, bite.

Prompt treatment of snake bites is essential – some bites, depending on the species, can be fatal. Veterinary treatment is essential. In the meantime, do not allow your dog to walk – it is better to carry it to your car in order to minimise the spread of the venom in the blood stream. Ants are also capable of giving a nasty sting if disturbed – treat as for wasps, etc.

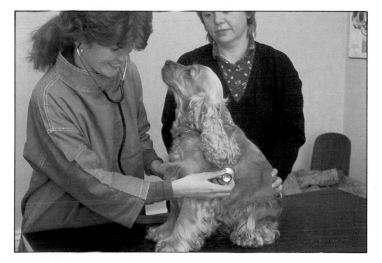

## Foreign bodies

Should your puppy or older dog
behave in an abnormal way with its
mouth, such as rubbing it along the
ground or pawing at it, it is possible
that the dog has something lodged
or trapped in or across its teeth –
usually halfway back. This is usually
the result of chewing a piece of
wood or a thin stick (or chop bone).
The throwing of sticks can be
dangerous, because sharp ends can
cause wounds at the back of the
throat. The best way to remove the
stick or bone if it is jammed is to
gently push it towards the back of
the mouth, where the distance
between the teeth is wider. In this
way, it will easily come free, but do
hold on to the offending item so as
not to let the dog swallow it. Most
people try to pull it to the front, but
this only makes matters worse, as it
becomes even more tightly fixed.

Should you have reason to think
that your dog has swallowed a small
ball or stone, then prompt action is
needed. It could be that the
windpipe is blocked, in which case if
nothing is done **immediately** the
animal will suffocate. Try to look to
see if the object is visible, in which
case try to release it with your
fingers. If not visible, administer
sharp blows to the ribs in an effort to
expel the air in the lungs, and in so
doing hopefully expel the object into
the dog's mouth. If you are
successful, then take the dog **at
once** for a veterinary check to see
that no damage has been done.

Another potentially dangerous
situation is the dog who has eaten a
substance or object which becomes
lodged at some point during its
journey through the digestive
system. The symptoms could
become obvious soon after the dog
has consumed the offending object,
or any signs may be delayed for days
or weeks. If in any doubt, consult
your veterinarian telling him as
much as you can if you suspect that
this could be the cause of your dog
being 'off colour'. Bones can
sometimes travel perfectly well
through the digestive tract, and then
cause a blockage near the anus,
needing expert attention to relieve

**Above:** *These toys are unsafe –
they can be easily chewed or
swallowed causing internal
obstruction or suffocation.*

**Right:** *When injections are given to
a puppy or nervous dog, it is
preferable to hold its head for
reassurance and control.*

the situation. Most likely things to
be swallowed are small balls, rubber
objects, round stones or peach
stones.

## Eclampsia

Possibly the next most urgent
condition after the above, as within a
matter of one or two hours you
could have a fatality. Eclampsia is a
condition associated with the brood
bitch and a large litter, usually when
her puppies are about three to four
weeks old. It is caused by too great a
strain on the calcium reserves of the
bitch. It can occur at any time, from
shortly before whelping up to when
the puppies are seven to eight
weeks old.

Treatment is by calcium injection,
subcutaneous or into the vein, by
your veterinarian, and is usually
miraculous in its effect. But do not
delay in getting to the veterinarian as
quickly as possible, as death can
occur at any time after the onset of
the symptoms. These are a glazed
look in the eyes, reluctance to walk,
pronounced panting, shaking and
trembling. If the bitch does try to
walk, she will only be able to
stagger. Vomiting can occur. If
these symptoms occur, telephone
your veterinarian **immediately**.

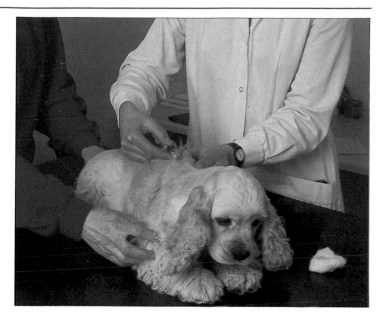

Prevention is possible in many cases by the introduction at the start of whelping (after one or two are born) of COLL-O-CAL D. Your veterinarian can supply this, and it should be continued, according to the instructions on the bottle, throughout lactation.

## SPECIFIC HEALTH PROBLEMS AND DISEASES

### Cystitis
This is quite common and, when it does occur, no doubt painful. Symptoms are frequent passing of urine, which is usually blood stained – not to be confused with the onset of a bitch's season, when she also urinates frequently. Veterinary treatment is essential.

### Bladder stones
These can can cause acute obstruction in dogs; retention of urine requires immediate veterinary attention. The symptoms are constant lifting of the leg and straining, with blood in the urine.

### Eczema
This skin condition is very often the result of other irritant conditions, such as parasites, anal glands that need attention or anything which causes the dog to scratch or nibble at its skin. Symptoms are the appearance of a hard, rather slimy wet patch, which is painful and very itchy, causing the dog to further aggravate it by scratching and nibbling. Do not ignore it and hope it will go away – it will not. Consult your veterinarian. He will have at his disposal the most effective and quick-acting drugs to deal with the condition. Prevention is better than cure – a parasite free and well-groomed dog is far less likely to suffer from Eczema.

### Grass seeds
During Summer and Autumn, these seeds can be a nuisance to long-eared breeds. If not detected, they will travel up the hair on the ear and then make their way down into the ear where they cause great discomfort and pain. Once out of sight, it is impossible for them to be removed except by a veterinarian, and in most cases this requires a general anesthetic. It is advisable, if you exercise your dog in fields or along grass verges, to inspect the ears during and after the walk to see if any of them are clinging to the hair, and removal is then possible.

**Above:** *The leg of a nylon stocking serves a dual purpose: to protect the ears from grass seeds and keep them clean at feeding time.*

However, if your dog starts to shake its head, or hang it on one side, it is most likely that a seed has gone right down into the ear. **Immediate** treatment is essential as the longer it remains in the ear the more damage it will do, and of course the pain is intense. Grass seeds also commonly penetrate the skin between the toes, and therefore paws should be inspected as well. Inter-digital cysts have a similar appearance (see below) and can be difficult to distinguish from grass seeds. Trimming long hair on ears and between pads and toes is the best method of prevention.

### Inter-digital cysts
These are not very common, but nevertheless worth a mention. Their cause is not known for sure, some dogs being more prone to them than others. The first sign is usually that the dog will pay a lot of attention to its front feet, particularly between the toes, with an abnormal amount of licking. Usually this leads to the appearance of a blister which swells and eventually bursts, discharging blood and pus, leaving a small hole which quickly disappears. The time taken for this to happen varies, but is usually a day or two. It can be very

painful to the dog and cause it to limp and resent you touching its foot. By all means mention this to your veterinarian, as he may suggest a course of treatment. But I have found, on the odd occasion when I have met this condition, that it resolves itself. It is unwise to force your dog to go for a long walk at this time.

### Kennel cough
This condition is usually picked up in boarding kennels or at shows. There is a vaccine recently developed, and some boarding kennels now insist on its administration prior to taking dogs into their care. In the average healthy dog, kennel cough is not a serious disease – rather like a mild influenza, accompanied by a persistent cough. Dogs seldom lose appetite, but exercise should be curtailed until the cough stops. This may take three to four weeks. Treatment is by antibiotics to suppress bacterial complications. However, in puppies and old dogs it can be more serious, so should you hear of any cases in the vicinity of your home be careful to avoid contact as it is highly infectious.

### Labial eczema
This is a nasty, smelly condition of the mouth, peculiar to Cockers, affecting the labial fold of skin on one or both sides. It can sometimes be treated topically, but may require surgery.

# Chapter Four

# BREEDING YOUR COCKER SPANIEL

Having considered the responsibilities of breeding a litter of puppies and deciding that you are prepared to undertake them, and being prepared for the hard work and expense which will be entailed in rearing the litter until it is eight weeks old, then you can go ahead and plan your breeding programme.

Plan is the operative word, for much thought is required beforehand. Breeding a litter is not just a matter of taking your bitch to the nearest dog of the same breed. You should be aiming to produce sound, quality puppies with excellent temperaments, taking the greatest care to steer clear of hereditary problems. The owner of the American Cocker bitch should arrange to have the bitch's eyes tested when she comes into season, prior to mating.

### Choosing a stud dog

It is imperative that the dog you choose is a sound, healthy, typical representative of its breed. Temperament is most important; steer away from nervous or aggressive dogs. Breed Club Secretaries can often furnish you with much helpful information and point you in the right direction.

Priority should be given to minimising the risk of hereditary problems. All responsible owners of American Cocker stud dogs have current eye clearance certificates

for clear dogs. You should ask to see these before arranging to use the dog. Enquire about his parents. Follow the advice offered in the sections on hereditary problems. The owner of the English Cocker bitch should also enquire about any occurence of FN in the stud dog's pedigree and seek advice on his or her own bitch's blood lines. Again, Breed Club Secretaries and serious breeders are usually only too willing to help in these matters.

The choice of stud dog will also depend on the reason for your breeding. If you merely want a litter of typical puppies, then the decision is simpler. You might be guided by colour preference or because you like a particular dog or dogs from a particular kennel. If you are wanting to breed a prospective show quality puppy and improve on your stock, then there are more complex, scientific principles which can be applied. There are three possible paths open to you.

### In-breeding

This is the mating of closely related dogs, such as father to daughter and brother to sister. In-breeding can produce beautiful stock, as it can fix desirable qualities in a strain. However, apart from 'doubling up' on desirable traits, in-breeding also doubles up on undesirable traits which may be lurking recessively. In-breeding is not recommended for the novice breeder.

## Line breeding

Line breeding is a more diluted form of in-breeding as it consists of the mating of related animals, but the common ancestor(s) may be two or three generations removed. The same benefits and drawbacks of in-breeding are applicable here, but to a lesser degree. Line breeding keeps the resultant progeny closer to the established type. It is important that the ancestor(s), which is common to both sides of the pedigree, is an outstanding individual, free from undesirable traits, as in line breeding you are establishing these traits in greater concentration into your line. The most successful kennels often base their breeding programmes on line breeding. When you hear someone remark of a particular kennel 'all their dogs look the same', the chances are that the stock is extensively line bred. It is the most successful way of establishing uniformity and 'type'.

In close line breeding, the same dog or bitch might appear five or six times in four or five generations. Line bred puppies have a greater chance of inheriting the characteristics of their ancestors.

## Outcrossing

This is the mating of unrelated dogs. Outcross mates are usually chosen in an attempt to improve a particular point, eg a dog with an outstanding head and from a bloodline which excels in this point might be chosen as a mate for a bitch with a poor head. When practising this type of mating it should be pointed out that the progeny of outcross matings are often less uniform in type than the progeny of line breeding. It is important also, when choosing a stud dog in this manner, that you try not to introduce undesirable traits into your bloodline, and never use a dog who has the same fault as your bitch.

## Preparations for mating

After your researching, you will have finally decided on a stud dog. It is wise to telephone the owner of the dog well before your bitch is due in season and ask if the dog would be available for your bitch. Some dogs are not at public stud; some are limited to approved bitches. Be prepared for the dog's owner to enquire about your bitch's pedigree. Responsible stud dog owners are very careful in vetting prospective mates for their dogs. The resultant progeny could enhance or damage a dog's reputation, so all risks are avoided. Enquire about the stud fee and the terms for mating. Most stud dog owners allow a free return if a bitch does not conceive, but it is wise to ask about this when making your arrangements.

When the bitch comes into season, arrange the dates for mating. The best time for mating varies with individual bitches. It is important to notice the first day when a bitch shows colour. The generally accepted days for readiness to mate and likely conception are the 11th, 12th and 13th days of the season, but some bitches will stand for a dog before and after these days. The most reliable signs are when the discharge from the vulva has become pale and the bitch is swinging her tail in readiness for mating.

Do ensure that your bitch is in peak condition before mating. You should worm her when she comes into season and ensure that she is not too fat, which not only makes mating difficult, but reduces the chances of conception.

## Mating

When a bitch approaches readiness for mating, she releases eggs which must be fertilized by the dog's sperm for pregnancy to occur. These eggs, on their release, may take hours or a couple of days before they are receptive to sperm. Because of this gradual ovulation process, it is sensible to arrange two matings for your bitch, on subsequent days or after a day's lapse. This will increase the chances of conception.

Although one mating is often sufficient to achieve conception, I personally think that whenever possible, a second mating is

**Above:** *A proud mother with her son, the product of a carefully planned mating. It is essential that only quality, sound and healthy stock is used in any breeding programme you undertake.*

sensible, especially when you have travelled many miles with your bitch.

Mating is not always as easy as it sounds, and whoever said that stud dogs bring easy money has led a narrow or lucky life! Stud dogs and their owners often have their own foibles at this time. Some dogs prefer to mate a bitch without human assistance; some will not perform if the bitch is held. Some owners will not allow their dogs to mate a bitch which is not securely held. Nervous bitches and over-anxious owners also complicate matters. Be prepared to assist the stud dog owner if required. On the other hand, do not be offended if you are asked to leave the room until the mating is accomplished. In this instance, most stud dog owners will be quite agreeable to you seeing 'the tie'.

Stud fees should be paid for at the time of mating and a receipt should be given. The stud dog owner should furnish you with a Kennel Club form for the registration of the resulting litter, with a signed statement of mating with the dog's Kennel Club registration number. When the litter is born, you should fill in the remaining sections with details of the dam, number, sex and colour of the pups and return the form to the Kennel Club with the correct fee. If the sire or dam is unregistered at the time of mating, this should be rectified immediately as it will prevent registration or showing of the progeny and also reduce their value.

### Whelping preparations

As the time for the birth of the litter (whelping) draws nearer, it is vital that you are well prepared. It is quite usual for bitches to whelp a few days before the expected date and it is important not to be caught out.

Most important are the whelping quarters. A specially made whelping box is advisable. There are various types commercially available but it is quite feasible to make your own. The box should be big enough for the bitch to turn around comfortably, leaving additional space so she does not have to trample over her puppies. It should be a stout timber

construction of about 3 ft (91.5cm) in length and 2½ft (76cm) wide and 2½ft high. A false bottom is useful, as it can be removed and scrubbed. It can also be covered in towelling or blanket which can be tucked under it. This rough surface is not only warm for the pups but aids them in their crawling and walking. It also minimises the risk of suffocation under loose blankets and towels. Some whelping boxes have hinged lids and fronts which can be used for extra warmth and security.

Save all your newspapers and old towels. They will be most useful during whelping and through the following weeks.

The siting of the whelping box is most important. Whether it is in an outside kennel, in your kitchen or a spare room in the house, one thing is vital: warmth. Particularly in the first two or three weeks of life, puppies need warmth to thrive. If the kennel or whelping box is unheated, then an infra red lamp suspended above the whelping box

**Below:** *A whelping box with many useful features, as labelled. The feet serve to raise the box above a possibly cold and damp floor and provide ventilation.*

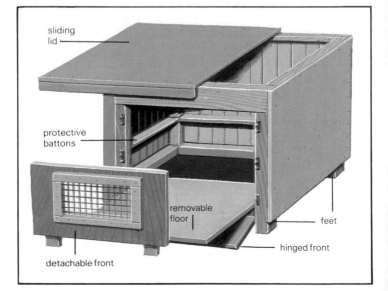

sliding lid

protective battons

removable floor

feet

hinged front

detachable front

should be used. There are also some commercially manufactured, electrically-heated whelping boxes which can be used.

It is advisable to introduce the bitch to her whelping quarters a week or so before the pups are due so she can accustom herself to her new surroundings.

## Coat care

For English and American Cockers, it will probably be necessary to reduce the amount of tummy feathering before whelping. If you are not planning to show the bitch for a long time then you can remove all the tummy coat, especially around the teats. If you want to retain some coat, then leave some of the coat on the flanks, but remove the central strip of hair from the abdomen, leaving all the teats clear of hair. Particularly long leg furnishings should be trimmed back also. It has been known for young pups to suffocate or be strangled through being caught up in this hair.

After the bitch has whelped, there will be a heavy, coloured mucous discharge from the vulva for several weeks after whelping. This can stain and mat the bitch's rear furnishings. To avoid this you can wash the bitch's hindquarters and rear furnishings with a mild disinfectant solution and gently brush out the furnishings. Some breeders find an oilated coat dressing also helps prevent matting and coat loss in this area.

## The in-whelp bitch

The normal gestation period for a bitch is 63 days. The first few weeks after mating are often a nail-biting time for owners, especially if they are new to breeding. There is often an impatient anxiety to know whether a bitch has 'taken', and if she is actually in whelp. Many owners, mistakenly in my opinion, take their bitches to the vet for his opinion on whether the bitch is in whelp. There is no need to do this; time will tell. The bitch will usually not show any signs of pregnancy until the fourth or fifth week after mating and often the first tell-tale

signs are temperamental rather than physical. The pregnant bitch may become calmer, more meditative and very affectionate. From about the fifth week the flanks begin to thicken out and the body begins to grow perceptively rounder. The teats enlarge at this stage and develop a pinkish hue. Some bitches, like humans, suffer from morning sickness at this stage.

Until the sixth week of her pregnancy, the bitch needs no change to her daily routine or diet. Pregnancy is no reason for reducing exercise; good muscle tone is important and will often help the bitch in whelping. As long as the bitch is normally well fed on red meat or tripe and a good quality biscuit, then she needs no supplementary feeding until the sixth week. From this time her appetite will usually increase and it is sensible to give her an extra meal. It is the extra protein which is important, so meat, poultry, fish and egg yolks can be increased.

I personally add vitamins and minerals to the pregnant bitch's diet, including a calcium supplement. All my dogs receive daily yeast tablets and cod liver oil, but I think they are especially important to the pregnant bitch's diet. The heavy in-whelp bitch often cannot manage big meals, but copes better with more frequent, smaller meals. By the eighth week, I feed my bitches three times a day.

## Whelping

The first signs that a bitch is going into labour are a general restlessness, shivering, a refusal of food and frequent bouts of panting. Some bitches may vomit during this stage. She will have a thick, clear mucous discharge from the vulva. This acts as lubrication in preparation for whelping. The bitch will begin scratching in a corner of her whelping box, ripping up newspapers and bedding. She is effectively making her nest or burrow for whelping. This stage of whelping can last many hours. The bitch's restlessness and discomfort are caused by the first mild contractions of the uterus.

As the uterine contractions increase in frequency and strength, the bitch will lie down, often stretching her rear legs to press against the walls of her whelping box. The strong contractions can be seen: a muscular tremor runs along the bitch. She may moan or cry out during these contractions, which are effectively pushing the whelp along the vaginal canal for the birth. If a bitch is having strong contractions for more than two hours and no puppy arrives, then you should consult your veterinarian without delay.

The first puppy is proceded by a water bag which breaks, and gives us the warning that the first puppy is about to be born. After a few minutes and a few more contractions, the whelp, in a membrane sac, is expelled, usually head first, from the vulva. The puppy must be removed from this sac, either by the bitch or, if she lacks the maternal instinct to do it, the owner. Often a bitch will do all that is necessary: breaking open the bag, biting through the umbilical cord and stimulating the puppy by licking it. If the bitch does not do it, then you must. Break open the bag; take hold of the umbilical cord about 2in (6cm) from the puppy's abdomen, drain the fluid in the cord towards the puppy and cut through the cord. The puppy should be rubbed vigorously with a warm rough towel to dry it and stimulate its circulation. Ensure that the puppy's nose and mouth are clear of mucous; a vigorous downward shake, holding the puppy firmly, will clear these passages to facilitate breathing and sucking.

Shortly after the pup is born, the bitch will expel the placenta or afterbirth. This is high in protein nourishment and she will have the natural instinct to eat this. However, with a large litter, eating all the afterbirths is likely to cause diarrhoea.

Whelping is a messy business. After each puppy is born and dried it is wise to clean up. Change the newspapers in the whelping box and offer the bitch a drink of milk, which she can take before contractions resume for the next puppy. The newly born pups will find their own way to a teat and will probably take their first milk. Once heavy contractions resume, however, great care must be taken that the puppy is not squashed or trampled by the bitch. Some breeders recommend that pups should be removed until whelping is finished, but I have always found that most bitches are very upset when their newly-born whelps are taken away and refuse to get on with the whelping. On one occasion, I placed six newly born pups into a shoebox while the bitch rested between contractions for another puppy. I left the room for a few minutes and returned to find the bitch nestled gently on top of the shoe box with six puppies unharmed underneath her!

Once the whelping is completed, take the bitch outside to relieve herself. On return, rub her down with a mild disinfectant solution which should be sponged on her rear parts, teats, nose and paws. Offer her a drink and then let her settle to enjoy her pups. Once you have ensured that all is well and they

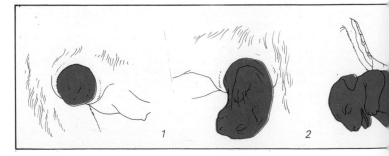

are feeding, she will benefit from peace and privacy. It is most unwise to allow lots of visitors to see dam and puppies during whelping and in the first weeks. She will resent intrusion, often even from her owner, and she will be very protective of her puppies.

## The first weeks

The day after whelping, it is wise to have your veterinarian call in to check over the bitch and her pups. He will ensure that the pups do not have any physical deformities, such as hare lips or cleft palates and he may give the bitch an antibiotic injection coupled with a drug to stimulate her milk supply.

For several weeks after whelping, it is quite natural for the bitch to have a discharge from the vulva. This discharge is dark at first but over the weeks turns to a pale pink mucous before finally ceasing. This discharge will stain and tangle the bitch's featherings unless rubbed down regularly. It is always useful to keep a bowl of diluted disinfectant solution and a sponge in the whelping room. The bitch may also be a little restless a few days after whelping. She may scratch up the papers in her whelping box or burrow in a corner.

---

Below: *The birth sequence.*
*1 The water bag containing the puppy appears at the vulva.*
*2 The puppy, still encased in the bag, emerges, usually head-first.*
*3 The bitch tears off the bag and gives the puppy a good wash.*
*4 The puppy's head is freed first so it can take its first breath.*

Cocker spaniels are usually excellent mothers and take excellent care of their pups. It is amazing to see the rate of growth of the pups over the first few weeks. They increase in weight quite rapidly. The routine of a healthy puppy is simple: feeding and sleeping. There is seldom any mess from a healthy litter. The dam will lick them to clean them, stimulate their circulation and encourage them to urinate and defecate. The puppies' eyes will open at about 10 days old.

## Post-whelping hazards

The breeder must watch his bitch, however, for the two most common post-whelping hazards: mastitis and eclampsia.

**Mastitis** This is caused by an excess of milk in the bitch. The teats become hard and painful for the bitch. Mastitis can be prevented by regular examination of the teats and gentle massage. It is a particularly common complaint when bitches have a small litter and have too much milk with some teats being hardly used. It is wise to use teats by rotation in these circumstances to ensure that there is no build up of milk. If the condition persists, it must be treated with antibiotics.

**Eclampsia** This is a much more serious condition, but happily much less common than mastitis. It is also known as milk fever and is caused by a shortage of calcium in the blood stream. It may occur just prior to, or just after, whelping but quite often about four weeks after whelping. The symptoms of eclampsia are

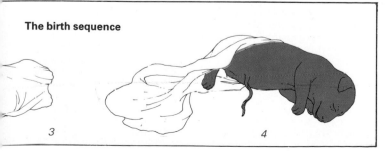

**The birth sequence**

3

4

dramatic and disturbing: the bitch will be restless and may shiver and vomit. The legs go stiff and the bitch may go into convulsions, her whole body twitching and becoming rigid. It is vital that the bitch receives veterinary treatment immediately. A long delay could mean losing the bitch. The vet will inject her with large quantities of calcium. The bitch usually recovers completely within hours but she should **not** be allowed to return to feed her litter as a relapse would be certain.

## Docking

At about four days old, the Cocker Spaniel puppy must have its dew claws removed and its tail docked, if desired. This is best left to the veterinarian or an experienced breeder.

## The nursing mother

The bitch nursing pups needs a much increased volume of food as there is a considerable drain on her resources. For the first day or so after whelping she might prefer a light diet of chicken or fish, but she will soon be able to return to a high protein, increased quantity diet. She should have water always available. I also offer the bitch regular drinks of milk and honey and increase her vitamin and mineral supplements and often add a little garlic to her main meals.

The well fed bitch will remain fit and in good condition whilst nursing and she is quite capable of rearing the puppies unaided for the first four weeks.

For the first few days the bitch will be unwilling to leave her puppies but she must be taken out regularly to relieve herself. After a couple of weeks she may be quite happy to go for short walks, but remember always to sponge her down before allowing her to return to her puppies. The English and American Cocker Spaniel will also benefit from being groomed once or twice a week. The bitch will lose quite an amount of feathering whilst nursing, but if regular brushing and combing of the whole coat is undertaken, heavy matting can be prevented.

## Weaning

Depending on the size of the litter and the condition of the dam, weaning of the puppies can usually be left until the fifth week. By this time the puppies will be walking around, albeit unsteadily. Spaniel puppies are usually very greedy and are weaned quite easily at this age.

The first attempts will be somewhat messy with more of the food ending up on the puppy's face than in its stomach, but it will soon learn. I tend to wean my litters on one of the many preparatory milk products such as *Lactol*, thickened with a baby cereal. I often add a little honey to this mixture. The puppy can be encouraged to lap by offering it a little of the mixture on a spoon, or on a well scrubbed finger. It will soon progress to its own saucer. Wean puppies individually at first, ensuring that each does know how to lap, then the litter can be allowed to feed from one or two bigger bowls. It is a very satisfying sight to see a litter, heads down, enjoying their first meal. The puppies can also be introduced to solid food at this age. They will usually be very keen on scraped red meat or very finely minced beef.

Over the following few weeks they should be introduced to a wide variety of suitable foods in preparation for their new homes. Rice puddings, scrambled eggs, cooked liver, chicken, pilchards, minced tripe, flaked and boiled fish, tinned dog food, are all acceptable, but should be introduced one at a time to the puppy's diet to avoid upsetting the digestive system.

Weaning is a gradual process. Once the puppies are accepting solid food they should still have opportunities of feeding from their mother. At first it is best to give the puppies one solid meal per day and gradually increase this as they become completely weaned. By the time the puppies are six weeks old the mother will be getting a little tired of them and glad of a break from them and will enjoy longer walks again. She should be fed away from the puppies as she may regurgitate her food for them. By

this stage, my bitches sleep with their puppies but only visit them for short spells during the day.

By the time your puppies are eight weeks old they should be completely weaned and on a diet of four meals per day. My puppies have milk and cereals for breakfast and supper with meals of meat/fish plus a fine puppy meal at noon and late afternoon. Vitamin and mineral supplements should also be included in one of the meals. A diet sheet should be passed on with the pedigree to the new owners when the puppies are sold. The number of meals is decreased but the size of them is increased as the puppy grows up.

## Worming

It is most important to worm the puppies at around five to six weeks of age. Roundworms are frequently found in puppies, but there are many excellent worming products on the market. Your veterinarian will also be able to supply you with worming

**Above:** *Fully weaned and in its new home, this puppy is feeding from a high-sided bowl which keeps its ears out of his food!*

medicine (see also pages 82-83 on parasites).

## Grooming

By six weeks of age, your Spaniel puppy will be looking like a miniature replica of its breed: its ears will be long, its head typically Spaniel and it will be developing featherings on its legs. Because of the often messy weaning procedure, and to prepare the puppy for later life, it is wise to get puppies accustomed to being brushed and combed, but gentleness is most important. It is also advisable to clip the puppies' nails, as they grow quite quickly and can cause soreness and pain to the dam whilst puppies feed from her. At this age, the nails are soft enough to be cut by sharp scissors or human nail clippers.

## Selling your litter

'I don't know how you can part with them' is a frequent remark passed by my friends whilst looking at a litter of puppies. Puppies at this age are certainly adorable: appealing, playful and lovable. But the breeder also knows that they provide a lot of hard work and that softens the blow of parting, plus the knowledge that the puppy is going to a home where it will be loved and appreciated as an individual.

If you have bookings for your puppies, all well and good, but if you have not, then you must advertise. Your local newspaper will usually carry an appropriate pet column. Your veterinarian may also have a notice board available in his surgery for such adverts. National dog papers and magazines are also most useful, especially for advertising show stock.

Not all prospective buyers are suitable as dog owners. The responsible, caring breeder should ensure that the puppy is going to a home where it will be cared for and loved. Owning an animal entails responsibilities and these should be pointed out: house training, exercise, veterinary bills, regular grooming, visits to the trimming parlour, seasons in bitches, boarding kennels during holidays – all should be mentioned. I am very wary of selling puppies to households where all of the family is out at work all day. Such isolation is no life for a dog, particularly during its puppyhood. I am also cautious in selling a puppy as a pet for the children, especially very young children who can be very rough and insensitive, and who can quickly grow tired of their playthings. I am horrified to see puppies advertised in the run up to Christmas as 'ideal Christmas presents'. To use a famous slogan: 'A dog is for life, not just for Christmas.'

If the buyers seem suitable then they should be furnished with a pedigree and a diet sheet. You should also inform them of local veterinary services and suitable trimming parlours. I always encourage buyers of my stock to contact me if they have any problems or queries and to let me know how their puppy settles in. There is no greater satisfaction than to receive letters or Christmas cards with photographs of dogs you have bred and who are now living happy lives as much loved family pets and companions.

Breeding sound, healthy dogs which add pleasure to other people's lives is an achievement of which to be proud, and should be the target at which breeders should aim.

**Below:** *Cocker Spaniel puppies are certainly adorable, but the breeder must impress upon buyers the care and attention they need.*

# Chapter Five

# SHOWING FOR THE NOVICE

M any people who buy a puppy 'only as a pet' then decide to show their handsome pet, only to be 'bitten by the bug' and embark on a pastime than can radically change their whole lifestyle!

The show world is a world apart, a hobby that can bring exciting moments and great thrills. But behind the glamour there is the need for constant work, dedication and perseverance. At the highest level, the show world is very competitive and critical. But despite the rivalry, which is the heart of any

competitive pastime, great and lasting friendships are invariably founded.

## THE UK SHOW SYSTEM

There are several types of show in the UK with varying degrees of qualification and competition.

Shows are divided into Variety Shows and Breed Shows. At a Variety Show, there may be individual breed classes, but more often than not your dog will have to take its chance in a mixed class such as A V Gundog (any variety of gundog) or A V Junior (for a dog of any breed under the age of 18 months). Breed Shows are run by individual breed clubs and cater only for that breed.

**Below:** *A judge examines a Cocker at an Exemption Show. These shows offer an informal atmosphere, ideal for the novice exhibitor.*

## Types of show
**Exemption** Many small country
agricultural shows or village fetes
feature such dog shows, catering
largely for local pet dogs with
classes for both pedigree and
non-pedigree dogs. Although
licensed by the Kennel Club, these
shows are exempt from nearly all KC
rules. Pre-show entry is not
required. They are usually casual,
friendly events designed to raise
funds for a local cause. They are a
good site for trying out the show
world.

**Sanction Shows** These are small
shows limited to 25 classes. Dogs
which have won major awards at
Championship and Open Shows are
not allowed to compete at Sanction
Shows.

**Limited Shows** These are limited to
members of the host society (it is
very inexpensive to become a
member). Again dogs who have
won awards towards the title of
Champion are ineligible.

**Open Shows** These are open to all
dogs, whether they are Champions
or not.

**Championship Shows** These are
open to all and the most competitive
of all types of show. It is at the
Championship Show that one is able
to win a Kennel Club Challenge
Certificate. These CCs, under three
different judges, bring the dog its
title of Champion, or Show
Champion for gundog breeds who
do not hold a field trial award.

There are usually classes for most
breeds at the general Championship
Shows. Breed classes are
sub-divided into classes for dogs
and bitches. The best dog is
awarded the dog CC, the best bitch,
the bitch CC and from these two the
judge decides the Best of Breed, a
much coveted award.

After breed judging, the Best of
Breed winner represents its breed in
the group judging. There are six
groups all together – the English and
American Cockers go forward to the
Gundog Group. The winner of this
then goes forward to the final Best
in Show judging to compete with
the other five group winners for the
supreme title of Best in Show –
something to dream about!

## Classes
The following is a list of typical
classes offered at Open and
Championships Shows.

**Minor puppy** For dogs of six and
not exceeding nine calendar months
of age on the day of the show.
**Puppy** For dogs of six and not
exceeding twelve calendar months
of age on the day of the show.
**Junior** For dogs of six and not
exceeding eighteen calendar
months of age on the day of the
show.
**Maiden** For dogs which have not
won a Challenge Certificate or a first
prize at an Open or Championship
Show. (Puppy, Special Puppy, Minor
Puppy and Special Minor Puppy
Classes excepted.)

**Below:** *Simon Briggs from Perth,
Australia, International Handler
1987 at Crufts Dog Show with the
American, Sh Ch Dizzy Dame.*

**Novice** For dogs which have not won a Challenge Certificate or three or more first prizes at Open and Championship Shows. (Puppy, Special Puppy, Minor Puppy and Special Minor Puppy Classes excepted.)

**Post Graduate** For dogs which have not won three Challenge Certificates under three different judges or seven or more first prizes in all at Championship Shows in Limit and Open Classes confined to the breed, whether restricted or not, at shows where Challenge Certificates were offered for the breed.

**Open** For all dogs of the breed for which the class is provided and eligible for entry at the show.

## THE US SHOW SYSTEM

### US Breed Specialty Shows

In the United States, the Cocker Spaniel (American) has three varieties within the breed,

categorized according to colour, as follows: Black Variety – solid colour Black, including Black and Tan; Any Solid Colour Other Than Black (ASCOB); and Parti-Colour Variety (see US Breed Standard for full classification of markings).

In the Breed Specialty Shows, the three varieties of Cocker Spaniel (American) are shown separately, the Best of Variety being awarded for each of the three varieties. In the case of the English Cocker, which has no varieties within the breed, the Best of Breed designation is given.

The classes offered are the same whether there are varieties within the breed, or not (see page 108 for a classification of classes), each class having four placements, from first to fourth. The classes are divided between dogs, which are shown first, and bitches, shown after the dogs. First place dogs compete again for Winners Dog, as do the first place bitches for Winners Bitch. Only Winners Dog and Winners Bitch may be awarded Championship points. The Winners will then compete against the 'specials' – Champions of record – for Best of Variety or Best of Breed.

*Below: A striking Black and White American Cocker competes at a Championship Show, where the coveted CCs are on offer.*

## Classes

The classes at specialty and all-breed shows are primarily the same.

**Puppy** For dogs of 6-12 months of age. The class may be divided into 6-9 months and 9-12 months.

**Novice** This class is for dogs at least six months of age that have not won a class except Puppy, and have not won more than three times in Novice.

**Bred by exhibitor** In this class, dogs must be shown by the breeder or co-breeder.

**American bred** For dogs of six months of age or older bred in the US.

**Open** For dogs at least six months of age, usually entered by more mature dogs. An imported dog must be entered in this class.

**Specials** For Champions of record. Both dogs and bitches are shown together in this class with the Winners Dog and Winners Bitch.

## US All-Breed Shows

At All-Breed Shows, the same classes are offered as for the Breed Specialty Shows. Each Best of Variety or Best of Breed is shown again in its group – the Sporting Group for the American and English Cocker Spaniels, the six other groups being Hound, Working, Terrier, Toy, Non-Sporting and Herding. There are four placements in each of the seven groups, the first place winners going on to complete for Best in Show.

## Matches

AKC sanctioned matches for pure-bred dogs competing on an informal basis are given by specialty and all-breed clubs. No Championship points are awarded. These events provide an excellent opportunity for clubs, exhibitors, stewards and those wishing to become judges to gain experience needed for licensed shows. Sometimes a club will give a puppy match, limiting the entry to dogs of 3-12 months of age. This is a good time to socialize your new puppy and gain some show-ring experience.

Obedience and Junior Showmanship classes may be offered at sanctioned or fun matches as well.

## Champions

A dog or bitch must gain 15 points under at least three different judges to become a Champion. Championship points are awarded to Winners Dog and Winners Bitch. The number of points awarded at each show will vary according to geographic location and the number of dogs entered. Each Champion must have won at least two major point shows. Both 'majors', as they are known, must be won under different judges.

**Below:** *An English Cocker being judged in the Gundog Group, Crufts 1987. The equivalent group in the US is the Sporting Group.*

## THE CONTINENTAL SHOW SYSTEM

In Europe, all dog shows are governed by regulations laid down by the FCI (Fédération Cynologique Internationale), with small national differences. Each country also has its own Kennel Club.

Basically there are two main types of show: championship shows and small, informal, fun shows, usually held by breed clubs.

### Judging

Judging takes the form of a written critique on each exhibit, graded excellent, very good, good or sufficient. This report is usually written on the spot and passed to the exhibitor. Judging, therefore, can be a lengthy process, but there are far fewer shows in Europe as well as fewer exhibits than in either the US or UK.

### Classes

Usually, classes are limited to Youth, Open and Championship, although additional classes are allowed. Periodically, there are Brace and Team classes. The Youth class limits exhibits by age, usually 9-24 months.

**Above:** *Show dogs must learn to be 'benched': the housing for dogs when not being exhibited. Line it with a rug or cushion; remember to bring a water bowl.*

### Awards

Only dogs awarded an excellent grading can be considered for the Best of Sex award. In some countries, the excellent grading is excluded from the Youth class.

Best of Breed is a fairly rare award in Europe. Consequently, there cannot be any group or Best in Show judging. Exhibits deemed to be of outstanding merit over and above the excellent grading may be awarded the CACIB (Certificat d'Aptitude au Championat International de Beauté) or the CAC Certificat d' Aptitude au Championat). The CACIB can only be awarded at international championship shows.

To become a champion, a dog must be awarded three certificates (CACIB or CAC) under two different judges, with at least a 12-month interval between the first and last certificates. These certificates can be won in any country affiliated to the FCI.

## YOUR FIRST SHOW

### Is your dog good enough?

If you are going to become seriously involved in the hobby of showing dogs, it is pointless to proceed unless your dog is of sufficient quality to promise a certain amount of success. Dog showing is a time-consuming hobby; it can also be costly. Your dog will need to be trimmed; so this means time or money. Then there are entry fees to pay and the cost of travel to the shows.

To engage in such expenditure of time and money without some chance of success would be a rather dispiriting pastime. Besides, it costs just as much to prepare and show a mediocre specimen as it does to show a Champion.

If you already have your Cocker Spaniel and want to find out if it has show potential, there are several ways in which you can do this. You could enter it for a local show and take pot luck! I do not really recommend this; until you know how to present and show your dog, it will be at a great disadvantage against others. It is much better to seek the opinion, help and advice of a breeder/judge of your breed. First contact the breeder of your dog. If he or she is inexperienced in this field, they might be able to point you towards someone who can help. Go to a local show, seek out a breeder and ask his or her advice. If he thinks the dog has potential, arrange a trim or a trimming lesson and seek out your local show dog training class.

Many local dog clubs run an evening training class to teach ring procedure to dog and owner. They are invaluable in socializing your dog, getting it accustomed to being examined and mixing with other dogs. It is here that the owner can learn the elementary skills of handling in the show ring.

**Below:** *An essential preparation for the show ring is to practise posing your Cocker on a table to show off its best points, for the judge's examination.*

### Making your entries

When entering your dog for its first show, choose a class suitable for its age and experience. The show schedule lists the classification and gives definitions and explanations of qualifications. Do not make the mistake of entering too many classes. Remember that you are both beginners so take it easy. You will learn much from your early experiences.

### Before the show

Having ascertained that your dog is of show quality and having learned the rudiments of show ring technique, it is important that you practice at home.

Your dog's deportment and stance are very important. Practice stacking (posing) your dog in a balance pose which shows off its

---

**Below:** *It is also important to practise moving your dog; a smart trot with the head held up is best to show off its movement. Keep the lead in your left hand.*

good points. Its front legs should be perpendicular under its body and parallel to each other. The dog's hind legs should be placed slightly behind its tail and slightly further apart than the front legs. Hold your dog's head under the chin, making the most of its neck and tucking any loose, unsightly skin into your hand. Do not obscure your dog's face with your hand. Your other hand should hold your dog's tail out at back level. Both of you will need practice at this and your dog should be trained to be patient and maintain this pose for a couple of minutes.

Next you should practice moving your dog. The best pace to show off its movement is a smart trot. Ensure that the dog keeps its head up; this is most important for its general balance and outline. Check the dog if it breaks into a gallop. You should keep your lead in your left hand. Walk in a straight line for about 10 yards, turn smartly, maintaining your dog on your left side and walk back. You should also practise moving your dog in a circle as you will be required to move your dog round the

ring (always in an anti-clockwise direction) and in a triangle. The triangular pattern enables the judge to see hind, front and profile movement.

As the show draws nearer you must ensure that your dog is in show condition: it should be well trimmed and groomed, neither too fat nor too lean, and should be bathed the day before the show.

You will find it essential to take your grooming equipment to the show for a last minute brush and comb before going into the ring. If you have a portable grooming table that will be most useful too.

**At the show**
Arrive in good time before the scheduled time for judging of your classes. This will allow you time to settle at the show and groom your dog. It will also give your dog the opportunity to accustom itself to the atmosphere of the show site.

Do not be nervous! Your nerves and tension will be transmitted down the lead and your dog will sense it and not produce its best performance. I have seen many 'strung-up' owners over-handle their dogs through show-ring tension.

When your class number is called by the ring steward, collect your dog's number and pin it to your lapel (in the US, you will be given an arm band bearing the number, which should be worn on the left arm). Then set your dog up for the judge's first examination. The judge will walk along the line of dogs taking in his or her first impressions. He will then ask the class as a whole to move round the ring. This is where your practice will come in useful. He will then examine each dog on the table. Whilst the dog before you is moving, place your exhibit on the table, and put it into the best position ready for the judge. Do not get between the judge and the dog. After the examination you will be asked to move in one of the patterns discussed previously. Do what the judge asks of you. You will then be able to return to your place amongst the other dogs until the individual examinations are completed. Praise your dog if it has done well. You can relax for a while. As the final dog is examined, give your dog a final brush up and then set it up in the correct stance. The judge will have a final look down the line and pick out the dogs he wishes to re-consider. If you are selected, proceed to the centre of the ring and set your dog up. If you are not selected, well, hard luck, accept the decision with good grace and leave the ring quietly. The judge may move his final selection

of dogs again before making his decision and then he will place them in order. Make a fuss of your dog; it has done its best for you. Accept your win or your loss with equal grace: there is always another day when the positions will be different.

If you find that you have enjoyed your first experience of showing, then it looks as if you might get the showing 'bug'. If you cannot relax to enjoy the show and its very special atmosphere, if you cannot bear losing, then forget it – showing is not for you.

Judging dogs is a highly subjective pastime. True, there is a breed standard which the judge should be applying, but each judge sees it in his or her own way. It is open to individual interpretation; hence one dog may be greatly admired by one judge whilst doing nothing for another judge. If you cannot accept such anomolies with philosophical reflection, then showing will do nothing for your blood pressure; better to stay away from the show ring and enjoy your Cocker Spaniel as a companion and friend.

**Left:** *Remember to take a basic grooming kit with you to the show to give your dog a last-minute brush and comb through.*

**Below:** *Cocker Spaniels being judged at the most famous dog show in the world, Crufts, 1987. The atmosphere is electric!*

# Appendix I

## The English Cocker Spaniel

### Breed Clubs

**United Kingdom and Republic of Ireland**
Black Cocker Spaniel Club: Hon Sec Mrs D Porter, Gristwood, Beech Hill Road, Headley, Hants, GU35 8DR.
Black Red or Golden Cocker Club of Ireland: Hon Sec Mr P Murphy, Auburndale, Grange, Maganey, Carlow, Eire.
Cheshire Cocker Spaniel Club: Hon Sec Mrs A Rathbone, 4 Harper Ave, Newcastle-under-Lyne, Staffs.
The Cocker Spaniel Club: Hon Sec Mr A E Simpson, Coltrim, Upper Pendock, Near Malvern, Worcs, WR13 6JW.
Cocker Spaniel Club of Ireland: Hon Sec Mrs Angi Arroll, 15A Grange Court, Marley Grange, Rathfarnham, Dublin 16, Eire.
Cocker Spaniel Club of Lancashire: Hon Sec Mrs D M Schofield, Cobbles, Norcot Brook, Near Warrington, Cheshire, WA4 4DX.
Cocker Spaniel Club of Scotland: Hon Sec Mrs E M Crichton, 148 Glasgow Road, Garrowhill, Glasgow G69 6EU.
Coventry Cocker Spaniel Club: Hon Sec Mrs M Allard, 49 Angela Avenue, Potters Green, Coventry.

The Devon and Cornwall Cocker Spaniel Club: Hon Sec Michael Owens, 299 Fort Austin Avenue, Crownhill, Plymouth.
Dublin Cocker Spaniel Club: Hon Sec Mr Wm McEntee, Dalkeith, Kilteeth Road, Kill, Nass, Co Kildare, Eire.
East Anglian Cocker Spaniel Society: Hon Sec Mrs O Norfolk, 'Tarlings', West Hanningfield, Near Chelmsford, Essex, CM2 8UU.
East of Scotland Cocker Spaniel Club: Hon Sec Mrs E Johnson, Knocktower, Newbridge, Midlothian, EH28 8NN.
Home Counties Cocker Spaniel Club: Hon Sec Mrs F Harness, Hillside, Colliers End, Ware, Herts, SG11 1EN.
Midland Cocker Spaniel Club: Hon Sec Mr R Pain, 57 New Inns Lane, Rubery, Birmingham B45 8TS.
North of England Cocker Spaniel Association: Hon Sec Mr B Taylor, Broom Cottage, Castle Road, Mow Cop, Stoke-on-Trent.
North Midlands and Eastern Counties Cocker Spaniel Club: Hon Sec Mrs W M Prince, Church Farm, Findern, Derbyshire.
North of Ireland Cocker Spaniel Club: Hon Sec

## The American Cocker Spaniel

### Breed Clubs

**The United Kingdom**
The American Cocker Club of Great Britain: Secretary, Mrs A M Jones, MBE, The Captain, Castle Morton, Malvern, Worcestershire.
The Home Counties American Cocker Club: Secretary, Mr W Bunce, 19 Garfield Road, Hailsham, East Sussex.
The Northern Counties American Cocker Club: Secretary, Mrs M F Slap, 66 Darbishire Road, Fleetwood FY7 6QA.

**The United States**
American Spaniel Club: Secretary, Mrs Margaret M Cieskowski, 12 Wood Lane, So Woodmere, NY 11598.
Cocker Spaniel Club of Arizona: Joy Ryan, 1002, Glenn Dr, Phoenix AZ 85020.
Bay Cities Cocker Spaniel Club: Mary B Cushman, PO Box 11, Alamo, CA 94507.
Cocker Spaniel Club of Orange County: Marieta McFarlane, 6543 Indian Trail Way, Fallbrook, CA 92028.
Cocker Spaniel Club of San Diego: Pam Kelly, 11650 Lakeshore Dr Unit 149, Lakeside, CA 92040.
Cocker Spaniel Club of Southern California: Ralfa Reveley, 7811 Shady Spring Drive, Burbank, CA 91504.
Mission Valley Cocker Spaniel Club: Roberta Denton, 18012 Via Rincon, San Lorenzo, CA 94580.
San Joaquin Valley Cocker Spaniel Club: Hylon Kaufmann, 1467 Holland, Clovis, CA 93612.
West Coast Cocker Spaniel Club: Linda Ciaravino, 1319 Glenclaire Dr, Walnut, CA 91789.
Greater Denver Area Cocker Spaniel Club: Denise Phelps, 1500 South Macon Street, Aurora, Colorado 80012.
Cocker Spaniel Club of Southeastern Florida: Mrs Gloria Bowman, 440 NE 10th Ave, Fort Lauderdale, Fl 33301.
South Atlantic Cocker Spaniel Club: Maryrose A Picciuolo, 4502 Ortega Farms Circle,

Jacksonville, Fl 32210.
Cocker Spaniel Specialty Club of Georgia: Nan Warren, 1550 Lackey Road, Woodstock, GA 30188.
Cocker Spaniel Club of Hawaii: Gerri Cadiz, 40-A Kai One P1, Kailua, HI 96734.
Cocker Spaniel Club of the Middle West: Kris Painter, 811 Oceola Dr, Algonquin, Il 60102.
Greater Peoria Cocker Spaniel Club: Peggy Underhill, 218 Anna Street, East Peoria, Il 61611.
Skyline Cocker Spaniel Club: Prudence Gaynor, 3114 N 77th Ave, Elmwood Park, Il 60635.
Salamonie Cocker Spaniel Club: Nadine Meyers, 1910 E Dupont Rd, Fort Wayne, In 46825.
Cocker Spaniel Club of Northwest Indiana: Mrs Judy Marchand, RT w Box 200z, Delphi, IN 46923.
Tall Corn Cocker Spaniel Club: Julia Kissell, 5829 SW 74th Street, Des Moines, IA 50321.
Cocker Spaniel Club of Kentucky: Mary Jo Sims, 181 Meadow Hill Dr, Bowling Green, KY 42101.
Cocker Spaniel Club of Greater New Orleans: James R Burse, 10900 Willowbrae Dr, New Orleans, LA 70124.
Capitol City Cocker Club: Linda Johnson, 3400 Slade Ct, Falls Church, VA 22042.
Cocker Spaniel Club of New England: Mrs Clair Ayer, PO Box 974, Belcher St, Essex, MA 01929.
Detroit Cocker Spaniel Club: Lois Fry, PO Box 241, Lake Orion, MI 48035.
Central Michigan Cocker Spaniel Club: Kay Brandhold, 13483 Horrell Rd, Fenton, MI 48430.
Hiawatha Cocker Spaniel Club: Jeanine Borash, 4326 Grimes Ave, N Robbinsdale, MN 55422.
Cocker Spaniel Club of Eastern Missouri: Denise Beaudoin-Aiken, 6922 Julian Ave, St Louis, MO 63130.
Heart of America Cocker Spaniel Club of Greater Kansas City: Lynn Wright, 13900 Sycamore Dr, Olathe, KS, 66062.
Ozarks Cocker Spaniel Club of Missouri: Sue Groves, RT 7, Box 374, Springfield, MO 65802.
Omaha-Council Bluffs Cocker Spaniel Club: Carol Halstead, 12967 Larimore Ave, Omaha, NE

Mr T J Gracey, BEM, 67 Knockvale Park, Belfast BT5 64J.
Parti-coloured Cocker Spaniel Club: Hon Sec Mr A Browne, 26 Grosvenor Road, Shipley, West Yorkshire.
Red and Golden Cocker Spaniel Club: Hon Sec Mrs V Hillary, Bidston, Nursery Lane, Hookwood, Horley, Surrey.
Rotherham and District Cocker Spaniel Club: Hon Sec Mrs A Richardson, 65 High Street, Bolton on Dearne, Rotherham, S Yorks.
South Wales and Monmouthshire Cocker Spaniel Club: Hon Sec Mrs E M Jones, 2 Springfield Close, Cwmback, Aberdare, Mid Glamorgan.
Ulster Cocker Spaniel Club: Hon Sec Mr Thos J Cardy, Mount Keepe, 36 Glen Road, Lower Castlereagh, Belfast, N Ireland.
West of England Cocker Spaniel Club: Hon Sec Mr A R Crocker, 36 Willis Road, Kingswood, Bristol BS 15 4SS.
Yorkshire Cocker Spaniel Club: Hon Sec Mr D W Shield, The Red House, Kirby Misperton, Malton, N Yorks Y017 0XL.

**The United States**
Cascade English Cocker Spaniel Fanciers: Beth McKinney, 909-208th Ave NE, Redmond, WA 98053.
English Cocker Spaniel Club of America. Secretary, Mrs Kate D Romanski, PO Box 223, Sunderland, Ma 01375.

English Cocker Spaniel Club of Southern California: Edyth Sawyer, 13520 Summit Knoll Rd, Agua Dulce, CA 91350.
Heart of Michigan English Cocker Spaniel Club: Jean Glassen, 4300 Stoll Rd, Lansing, MI 48906.

## Further reading

*The Cocker Spaniel*, V Lucas-Lucas, Popular Dogs Ltd, UK.
*The Cocker Spaniel*, J de Casembroot.
*The Cocker Spaniel*, Kay Doxford, South Group Ltd, UK.
*Cocker Spaniels*, H S Lloyd, Foyles Handbooks, London.
*The Spaniel Owner's Encyclopedia*, J Gordon, Pelham Books Ltd, UK.
*Cocker Spaniels*, Ian Harman, Williams and Norgate Ltd, London.
*Cocker Spaniels*, edited by Joe and Liz Cartledge, Ebury Press, UK.
*Cocker Spaniels*, V A H Matthews, Oxford University Press, UK.

**General:** *The Evans Guide for Counseling Dog Owners*, Job Michael Evans, Howell Book House Inc, New York.
*Happy Dog/Happy Owner*, M Siegal, Howell Book House Inc, New York.
*Training Your Dog*, Joan Palmer, Salamander Books Ltd, London.

68164.
Cocker Spaniel Club of New Jersey: Doris Peers, 2 Terry Ct, Montvale, NJ 07645.
Southern New Jersey Cocker Spaniel Club: Joan Adams, 832 Columbus Street, Burlington, NJ, 08016.
Capital District Cocker Spaniel Club of New York: Deborah Abrams, 17 Hitchins Rd, Saratoga Springs, NY 12866.
Carolina Cocker Club: Jeanne Smith, 644 Rock Creek Rd, Chapel Hill, NC 27514.
Cocker Spaniel Club of Central Ohio: Eunice Reed, PO Box 218-3915, US Rte 40 SE, West Jefferson, OH 43162.
Cocker Spaniel Club of Northern Ohio: Geraldine Drayer, 3528 Clayton Dr, North Olmsted, OH 44070.
Ohio Valley Cocker Spaniel Club: Wilma Parker, 9 Pinehurst Ct, Fairfield, OH 45014.
Cocker Spaniel Club of Central Oklahoma: Deborah Powell, RT 4 Box 150, Tuttle, OK 73069.
Cocker Spaniel Club of Tulsa: Richard Shackelford, 6719 S Troost, Tulsa, OK 74136.
Fort Vancouver Cocker Spaniel Fanciers: Sandra Smith, 18210 N F Cramer Rd, Battle Ground, WA 98604.
Keystone Cocker Spaniel Club: Deborah Gunkle, 26 Park Ave, Pine Creek Apt D 53, Chalfont, PA 18914.
Cocker Spaniel Club of Rhode Island: Hazel O'Rourke, 16 Henry St, Cranston, RI 02905.
Cocker Spaniel Club of Chattanooga: Janice Ridge, 29 Vista Dr, Chattanooga, TN 37411.
Cocker Spaniel Club of Memphis: Teresa Milliara, 2973 Windemere Dr, Memphis, TN 38128.
Cocker Spaniel Club of Knoxville/Nashville: Kathryn Houser, 714 Concord Rd, Concord, TN 37923.
Cocker Spaniel Club of Austin: Joan Alfred, 307 Yurnstone, Buda, TX 78610.
Beaumont Cocker Spaniel Club: Mable Brader, 8803 Crest Ridge Circle, Austin, TX 78750.
Cocker Spaniel Club of San Antonio: Patricia Joubert, 8538 Bristlecone, San Antonio, TX 78240.
Cocker Spaniel Club of South Texas: Donna Halbardier, 4239 Mossy Oaks, West Spring, TX 77389.
Cocker Spaniel Speciality Club of Dallas: Monty

Barbar, 3508 Cresent Dr, Dallas, TX 75205.
Lone Star Cocker Speciality Club: J Napper, 6048 Rickee Dr, Fort Worth, TX 76148.
Sun City Cocker Spaniel Club: Sharon Celum, 3209 McLean, El Paso, TX 79936.
Corpus Christi Cocker Spaniel Club: Carol Timerina, PO Box 681, Portland, TX 78374.
Spaniel Breeders Society: Mrs William Brainard Jr Vermont, RT 1 Box 25-G, Marshall, VA 22115.
Washington State Cocker Spaniel Club: Nancy Hurja, 15544 11th NE, Seattle, WA 98155.
Fanciers' Cocker Spaniel Club of Southern Wisconsin: Susan Roche, 3405 E Terra Cotta Ave, Crystal Lake, Il 60014.

## Further reading
*The New Cocker Spaniel*, Ruth M Kraeuchi, Howell Book House Inc, New York.
*The Complete Cocker Spaniel*, Milo G Delinger, Delingers, USA.
*The Cocker Spaniel*, Ella B Moffit, Orange Judd Publishing Co, New York.
*Breeding Better Cocker Spaniels*, A Grossman, Delingers, USA.
*Hereditary Cataract in the American Cocker Spaniel*, Dr F G Startup, *American Cocker Club of Great Britain Eye Compendium No 8*, UK.
*Inherited Ocular Diseases in the American Cocker Spaniel*, P G C Bedford, *American Cocker Spaniel Club of Great Britain Eye Compendium No 9*, UK.
**General:** *Dogs and How to Breed Them*, Hilary Harmar, Gifford, UK.
*A Dog of Your Own*, Joan Palmer, Salamander Books Ltd, London.

## Author's Acknowledgments
I am indebted to many people for helping in the production of this work. I wish to thank: Mrs A M Jones, MBE, Secretary of the American Cocker Club of Great Britain, for her encouragement and the loan of two very special books; Rick Beauchamp of the famous Beau Monde Kennels in the USA for his help and advice; Joan Rock, my faithful and super-efficient typist and proof-reader; Yvonne Knapper, Eileen Streich; and my dogs for giving me much pleasure and success, and the experience to write this work.

# Appendix II

## Useful Addresses

### Kennel Clubs
**Australia** Australian National Kennel Council, Royal Show Grounds, Ascot Vale, Victoria (Incorporating: The Canine Association of Western Australia; North Australian Canine Association; The Canine Control Council (Queensland); Canberra Kennel Association; The Kennel Control Council; Kennel Control Council of Tasmania; The RAS Kennel Club; South Australian Canine Association.)
**Canada** Canadian Kennel Club, 2150 Bloor Street West, Toronto M6S 1M8, Ontario
**France** Societe Centrale Canine, 215 Rue St Denis, 75083 Paris, Cedex 02
**Germany** Verband für das Deutsche Hundewesen (VDH), Postfach 1390, 46 Dortmund
**New Zealand** Kennel Club, Private Bag, Porirua.
**South Africa** Kennel Union of Southern Africa, 6th Floor, Bree Castle, 68 Bree Street, Cape Town 8001, S. Africa, PO Box 11280, Vlaeberg 8018
**United Kingdom** The Kennel Club, 1-4 Clarges Street, London W1Y 8AB
**United States of America** American Kennel Club, 51 Madison Avenue, New York, NY 10010.

## General

### The United Kingdom
**The Agility Club** The Spinney, Aubrey Lane, Redbourn, Hertfordshire AL3 7AN
**British Field Sports Society** 59 Kennington Road, London SE1 7PZ
**British Small Animals Veterinary Association** 7 Mansfield Street, London W1M 0AT
**British Veterinary Association** 7 Mansfield Street, London W1M 0AT
**Groomers Association** Uplands, 151 Pampisford Road, South Croydon, Surrey CR2 6DE
**Joint Advisory Committee on Pets in Society** Walter House, 418-422 The Strand, London WC2
**National Canine Defence League** 1 Pratt Mews, London NW1 0AD
**National Dog Owners' Association** 39-41 North Road, Islington, London N7 9DP
**People's Dispensary for Sick Animals** PDSA House, South Street, Dorking, Surrey
**Pet Food Manufacturers' Association** 6 Catherine Street, London WC2B 5JJ
**Pet Industry Association** 1 Lily Place, Saffron Hill,

## Glossary of dog terminology

|  |  |
|---|---|
| Action: | The way a dog moves. |
| Almond eye: | The eye set in an almond-shaped surround. |
| Angulation: | Angle formed by the bones, mainly the shoulder, forearm, stifle and hock. |
| Anorchid: | Male animal without testicles. |
| Anus: | Anterior opening under the tail. |
| Apple head: | An irregular roundedness of the topskull. |
| Apron: | The long hair on the throat and below the neck. |
| Backline: | Topline of dog from neck to tail. |
| Balance: | Correctly proportioned animal with correct balance, with one part in regard to another. |
| Barrel ribs: | Ribs which are so rounded as to interfere with the elbow action. |
| Bitch: | Female dog. |
| Brace: | Two dogs of the same breed. |
| Brace Class: | A class for two exhibits of the same breed owned by one person. |
| Brisket: | The forepart of the body below the chest between the forelegs. |
| Brood bitch: | Female used for breeding. |
| Canine: | Animal of the genus canis which includes dogs, foxes, wolves and jackals. |
| Canines: | The four large teeth in the front of the mouth, two upper and two lower next to incisors. |
| Carpals: | Bones of the pastern joints. |
| Castrate: | To surgically remove the testes of a male. |
| Chest: | Part of the body or trunk enclosed by ribs. |
| China eye: | A clear blue eye. |
| Chiselled: | Clean cut in the head, particularly beneath the eyes. |
| Close-coupled: | A dog comparatively short from ribs to pelvis. |
| Coarse: | Skull heavy in bone, wedge-shaped in muzzle. |
| Cobby: | Short-bodied, compact. |
| Conformation: | The structure and form of the framework of a dog in comparison with the requirements of the Breed Standard. |
| Cow-hocked: | Hocks turned inwards. |
| Crossbred: | The progeny of purebred parents of different breeds. |
| Croup: | The back part of the back above the hind legs. |
| Crown: | The highest part of the head: the top of the skull. |
| Cryptorchid: | A male dog with neither testicle descended. |
| Cull: | To eliminate unwanted puppies. |
| Culotte: | The feathery hair on the backs of the legs. |
| Dam: | Mother of the puppies. |
| Dew claw: | Extra claw on the inside lower portion of legs. |
| Dishface: | Nose higher at the end than in the middle or at the stop. |
| Dock: | To shorten the tail by cutting. |
| Dome: | The rounded part of the skull. |
| Double coat: | Undercoat plus outer longer coat. |
| Down faced: | Tip of nose below level of stop. |
| Down in pastern: | Weak or faulty pastern (Metacarpus), ie forelegs bent at pastern. |
| Drive: | Good thrust of rear quarters. |
| Dudley nose: | Brown or light brown nose. |
| Elbow: | The joint at the top of the forelegs. |
| Elbows out: | Elbows pointing away from the body. |
| Entropion: | A condition in which the eyelid turns inward and the lashes irritate the eyeball. |
| Expression: | The general appearance of all features of the head as viewed from the front and as typical of the breed. |
| Feathering: | Long, fine fringe of hair seen on the ears, legs, tail and body. |
| Femur: | The large heavy bone of the thigh between the pelvis and stifle joint. |
| Fiddle face: | An elongated, pinched-in foreface. |
| Fiddle front: | A crooked front out at elbow, pasterns close and feet turned out. |
| Flank: | Side of the body between the last rib and the hip. |
| Forearm: | Front leg between elbow and pastern. |
| Foreface: | Front part of the head before the eyes; the muzzle. |
| Frill: | Long hair under the neck and on the forechest. |
| Fringes: | The featherings. |
| Gait: | A style of movement, eg running or trotting. |
| Hackney action: | Front feet lifted high in action. |
| Hard-mouthed: | Given to biting down hard on retrieved game: a serious fault. |
| Hare foot: | A long narrow foot. |
| Haw: | A third eyelid at the inside corner of the eye. |
| Heat: | An alternative word for 'season' in bitches. |
| Height: | Vertical measurements from withers to ground. |
| Hindquarters: | Rear assembly of dog: pelvis, thighs, hocks and paws. |
| Hock: | Lower joint of the hindlegs. |
| Hocks well let down: | Hock joints close to the ground. |
| Hucklebones: | Top of the hip bones. |
| Humerus: | Bone of the upper arm. |
| In-breeding: | The mating of closely related dogs of the same standard. |
| Incisors: | Upper and lower front teeth between the canines. |
| Ischium: | Hipbone. |
| In season: | On heat; ready for mating. |
| Interbreeding: | The breeding together of different varieties. |
| Jowls: | Flesh of lips and jaws. |
| Layback: | The angle of the shoulder blade compared with the vertical. |

London EC1
**The Pet Trade Association Ltd.** 151 Pampisford Road,
South Croydon, Surrey CR2 6DE
**The Royal Society for the Prevention of Cruelty to
Animals** RSPCA Headquarters, Causeway, Horsham,
Sussex RH12 1HG

**The United States**
**American Animal Hospital Association** 3612 East
Jefferson, South Bend, Indiana 46615
**American Society for the Prevention of Cruelty to
Animals** 441 East 92nd Street, New York, New York
10028
**American Veterinary Medical Association** 930 North
Meacham Road, Schaumburg, Illinois 60196
**Animal Welfare Institute** PO Box 3650, Washington
D.C. 20007
**The Fund for Animals** 140 West 57th Street, New York,
New York 10019
**National Dog Groomers Association** PO Box 101,
Clark, Pennsylvania 16113
**The National Dog Registry** 227 Stebbins Road, Carmel,
New York 1051
**Orthopaedic Foundation for Animals** 817 Virginia

Avenue, Columbia, Missouri 65201
**Owner Handler Association of America** 583 Knoll
Court, Seaford, New York 11783
**Pet Food Institute** 1101 Connecticut Avenue N.W.,
Washington D.C. 20036
**Tatoo-A-Pet** 1625 Emmons Avenue, Brooklyn, New York
11235

# Magazines
**The United Kingdom**
*The Kennel Gazette*, 1-5 Clarges Street, Piccadilly,
London W1Y 8AB.
*Dog World*, 9 Tufton Street, Ashford, Kent TN23 1QN.
*Our Dogs*, Oxford Road, Station Approach, Manchester.
*Dogs Monthly*, Unit One Bowen Industrial Estate,
Aberbargoed, Bargoed, Mid-Glamorgan, CF8 9ET.

**The United States**
*The American Cocker Magazine*, 3074 Trinity Drive, Costa
Mesa, CA 92626.
*Dog World Magazine*, 300 West Adams Street, Chicago, Il
60606.
*Pure-Bred Dogs/American Kennel Gazette*, 51 Madison
Avenue, New York, NY 10010.

| | |
|---|---|
| Leather: | The flap of the ear. |
| Level bite: | The upper and lower teeth edge to edge. |
| Line breeding: | The mating of related dogs within a line or family to a common ancestor, ie dog to grand-dam or bitch to grand-sire. |
| Litter: | The pups from one whelping. |
| Loaded: | Superfluous muscle. |
| Loin: | Either side of the vertebrae column between the last rib and hip bone. |
| Mate: | The sex act between the dog and bitch. |
| Milk teeth: | First teeth. (Puppies lose these at four to six months.) |
| Molars: | Rear teeth. |
| Molera: | Incomplete ossification of the skull. |
| Monorchid: | A male animal with only one testicle in the scrotum. |
| Muzzle: | The head in front of the eyes, including nose, nostril and jaws. |
| Occiput: | The rear of the skull. |
| Oestrum: | The period during which a bitch has her menstrual flow and can be mated. |
| Out at elbow: | Elbows turning out from the body. |
| Out at shoulder: | Shoulder blades set too wide, hence just out from the body. |
| Out-crossing: | The mating of unrelated individuals of the same breed. |
| Overshot: | Front teeth (incisors) of the upper jaw overlap and do not touch the teeth of the lower jaw. |
| Pace: | The left foreleg and left hindleg advance in unison, then the right foreleg and right hindleg, causing a rolling movement. |
| Pads: | The tough, cushioned soles of the feet. |
| Paper foot: | A flat foot with thin pads. |
| Parti-colour: | A term used for a dog of two colours in equal proportion. |
| Pastern: | Foreleg between the carpus and the digits. |
| Patella: | Knee cap composed of cartilage at the stifle joint. |
| Pedigree: | A written record of the names of a dog's ancestors going back at least three generations. |
| Pelvis: | Set of bones attached to the end of the spinal column. |
| Pigeon-toed: | Forefeet inclined inwards. |
| Progressive Retinal Atrophy (PRA): | A hereditary defect of the eyes causing early loss of sight. |
| Puppy: | A dog up to 12 months of age. |
| Purebred: | A dog whose sire and dam belong to the same breed and are themselves of unmixed descent since the recognition of the breed. |
| Quality: | Refinement and finesse. |
| Quarters: | The two hindlegs. |
| Roach back: | A convex curvature of the back towards the loin. |
| Roan: | A mixture of white with another colour in equal proportions. |

| | |
|---|---|
| Saddle back: | Over-long back, with a dip behind the withers. |
| Scapula: | The shoulder blade. |
| Scissor bite: | The outside of the lower incisors touches the inner side of the upper incisors. |
| Second thigh: | The part of the hindquarters from stifle to hock. |
| Set on: | Insertion or attachment of tail or ears. |
| Set up: | Posed so as to make the most of the dog's appearance for the show ring. |
| Sickle-hocked: | Unable to straighten the hock joint on the back reach of the hind leg. |
| Sire: | A dog's male parent. |
| Snipy: | Muzzle pointed and weak. |
| Spay: | To surgically remove the ovaries to prevent conception. |
| Splay feet: | Feet with toes spread wide. |
| Spring: | The roundness of ribs. |
| Standard: | A word picture of a breed in type and style. |
| Sternum: | The brisket or breast bone. |
| Stifle: | The hindleg above the hock. |
| Stop: | Indentation between the eyes. |
| Straight in shoulder: | The shoulder blades straight up and down as against laid back. |
| Stud: | Male used for breeding. |
| Stud Book: | A record of pedigree, age, name, breeder and owner of all the recognised breeds. |
| Sway back: | A sagging back. |
| Tail set: | How the base of the tail sets on the rump. |
| Thigh: | Hindquarters from hip to stifle. |
| Throatiness: | An excess of loose skin under the throat. |
| Topline: | The dog's outline from just behind the withers to the tail set. |
| Tricolour: | A term used when dogs have three colours more or less proportionate. |
| Trousers: | The hair on the hindquarters. |
| Turn-up: | An up-tilted foreface. |
| Type: | The characteristic qualities distinguishing a breed; the embodiment of a standard's essentials. |
| Undershot: | The front teeth of the lower jaw projecting or overlapping the front teeth of the upper jaw. |
| Upper arm: | The humerus or bone of the foreleg between shoulder blade and the forearm. |
| Vent: | The anal opening. |
| Weaving: | The crossing of the front or hindlegs when in action. |
| Well let down: | Having short hocks. |
| Well-sprung ribs: | Roundness or curvature of the rib cage. |
| Whelp: | An unweaned puppy. |
| Whelping: | The act of giving birth. |
| Withers: | The highest point of the shoulders just behind the neck. |
| Wry mouth: | Lower jaw does not line-up with upper jaw. |